What About the Workers?

Getting the best from employee surveys

Mike Walters was educated at Nottingham High School and Queens' College, Cambridge. He subsequently completed a post-graduate Diploma in Personnel Management, and he is a corporate member of the Institute of Personnel Management. He has worked in personnel and employee relations for Shell and the BBC. Between 1987 and 1989 he was Manager – Organization and Human Resource Planning for the IPM. He was a co-author of the IPM publication, *Changing Culture: New Organizational Approaches*, published in 1989.

Mike Walters is currently a Human Resources Consultant with ER Consultants in Cambridge.

What About the Workers?

Getting the best from employee surveys

Mike Walters

Institute of Personnel Management

Phototypeset by Input Typesetting Ltd, London and printed in
Great Britain by Short Run Press Ltd, Exeter, Devon.

British Library Cataloguing in Publication Data
Walters Mike
  What about the workers?
  1. Business firms. Attitudes of personnel. Surveys
  I. Title   II. Institute of Personnel Management
  658.315

  ISBN 0–85292–445–3

Cover design by Fred Price
Cover photograph from 'Modern Times'
supplied by The Kobal Collection Ltd.

The views expressed in this book are the author's own, and may
not necessarily reflect those of the IPM.

Contents

Acknowledgements

Most of what follows is my own fault. However, one or two people deserve thanks and recognition, if only for tolerance. First, thanks to my colleagues in ER Consultants, for their encouragement, advice, anecdotes and the use of material from the ER Cambridge Resource Centre. Second, thanks to Anne Cordwent, my Commissioning Editor at the IPM, for getting me to do this in the first place (and for making sure it got done at all – I've rarely been nagged so charmingly). Third, and most of all, thanks to Christine, for the support, encouragement, ideas, cups of coffee, glasses of wine, and everything else.

Introduction

'Evil communications corrupt good manners'

1 Corinthians xv. 33

There's an old joke about the Lone Ranger pursuing a bunch of bank robbers who have fled town in a stagecoach. Together with Tonto, he follows the trail of the stagecoach until they lose it in the desert.

The Lone Ranger, never at a loss in such circumstances, says, 'We'll split up. You go that way and I'll go this. Don't forget, keep your ear to the ground and use your Indian tracking skills.'

'Okay, Kemo Sabe,' says Tonto, and so they ride off in their different directions.

The Lone Ranger circles round for an hour or so, but sees no sign of the stagecoach. Eventually he decides to return to the area where Tonto's been hunting. After a while he sees Tonto in the road ahead, kneeling with one ear pressed to the ground. 'Tonto,' he calls, 'I'm glad to see you're using your Indian tracking skills. Do you know where the robbers are?'

'Yes, Kemo Sabe,' says Tonto, 'the stagecoach passed this way not fifteen minutes ago. There were three robbers, two wearing black hats and the third wearing a red bandanna. The stagecoach was painted blue and had four horses, three brown and one black.'

'That's incredible, Tonto,' says the Lone Ranger. 'How could you possibly know all that?'

'Because,' says Tonto, patiently, 'they drove over my head.'

Tonto's experience seems to have had a profound influence on management practice over the years. There are still many managers who are nervous about putting their ears to the ground in case they get their heads trampled in the process. For these

1

managers, communication, if it happens at all, is a one-way process. They talk down to their employees, and make every effort to avoid listening to the messages coming up from below.

Of course, these managers have lots of plausible excuses to justify their deafness. They argue that they've been doing their jobs effectively enough for years, thank you, without worrying about what their employees were thinking. Or they argue – sometimes in the same breath – that they *already* know quite enough. After all, they say, we meet them every day, have lunch with them occasionally, share some cheap red wine at the office party. And in any case, they go on (still without taking a breath), if we start *asking* them what they think, who knows where it'll end? It'll only encourage the bolshie ones to start stirring up trouble, won't it?

These kinds of attitudes are still common. They linger among supposedly enlightened managers brought up on a steady diet of *In Search of Excellence* and Total Quality Management. They linger even among managers who in theory are fully in favour of staff consultation, who thoroughly support worker participation and who can recite the contents of the EC Social Charter in their sleep.

The problem is that all communications involve an element of risk. And encouraging others to give their views is an even more risky business. The process may open up issues we would prefer to stay closed. It may raise expectations we would rather not fulfil. It may arouse interest in subjects we've previously managed to ignore. It may even encourage personal attacks on ourselves or our past actions. At best the process is likely to be a profound irritation to any manager – and this includes most of us – who prefers a quiet life.

Just to prove the point, the press recently carried a story about an employee survey commissioned by a large company with major industrial-relations problems. The survey was initiated by the Personnel Director and carried out, perfectly properly, by a team of external researchers. The survey results indicated that morale in the organization was very low. Furthermore, there was a high level of dissatisfaction with working methods, management style and a host of other human-resource issues. Worse still, the results suggested that the primary cause of these dissatisfactions was the company's Chief Executive, a highly dominant and outspoken individual. The Chief Executive was widely viewed as autocratic, aggressive, rude, domineering and, worst of all, not even particularly competent. To cap it all, there was a widespread belief that the survey would serve no useful purpose because the Chief Executive would accept no criticism.

Eager to provide confirmation of this view, the Chief Executive quickly suppressed the results of the survey. The team of researchers was dismissed before their study was complete, the Personnel Director was swiftly eased out and copies of the offending report were pulped. The only trace of the exercise, apart from the one copy leaked to the press, was the intense discontent of a workforce which had seen its hopes of change momentarily raised only to be utterly dashed. Readers will probably not be unduly surprised to learn that industrial relations in the company did not improve.

Given this kind of experience, it's perhaps not surprising that many managers fight shy of seeking their employees' views. After all, look at the poor Personnel Director in that story – what's the point of encouraging that kind of outcome? Life's tricky enough as it is. Far better to let things ride, just as they always have. We've managed all right up to now.

So why consult employees?

Unfortunately, complacency is no longer possible. It's already a cliché to say that 'people are our most important asset' or that 'our employees are our most important resource', but like most clichés it's also generally true. In a world of increasingly unpredictable markets, dramatically changing technology and ever faster communications, business performance is more and more determined by how flexibly and effectively we can use our human resources. And the effective management of our human resources – through our organizational structures, management style, recruitment, training, reward and all the other elements of personnel activity – is likely to be influenced strongly by how well we understand our employees' needs, motives and desires.

At the same time, the harassed manager's traditional excuses for not seeking employees' views no longer hold water (assuming they ever did). You may have managed quite well in the past without knowing what your employees were thinking. That doesn't mean you will in the future. As human resource management becomes ever more critical, you will need to know *why* your employees are not performing as effectively as they might. If reward strategies become increasingly individualized and performance-based, you will need to know exactly *what* is likely to motivate your workforce. As change becomes an increasingly common fact of life, you will need to know *how* change can most swiftly and painlessly be accomplished.

Furthermore, managers cannot simply assume that they already know the answers to these kinds of questions. They may well meet their employees over lunch every day, but that doesn't mean that their employees will always tell the truth – and certainly not the whole truth. It takes a brave person to criticize the boss to his or her face. It takes a fairly brave person to make adverse comments about *any* aspect of the organization unless they're fairly sure the boss is going to agree. The odd person who does speak his or her mind – perhaps after a few too many at the office party – often lives to regret it. The boss takes a tougher line in future, those occasional late arrivals or early departures are no longer tolerated, career opportunities mysteriously disappear.

No, in general, people at work temper honesty with diplomacy. And even in comparatively non-contentious areas, managers often base their actions and decisions on ill-founded assumptions. If the company or department is considering relocating, for instance, it's all too common for managers to say, 'Oh yes, of course George'll come with us. He's always talking about moving out of London.' They fail to realize that, while George may indeed *talk* about moving out of London, it's really the last thing he wants to do. On the other hand, the manager might say, 'Mary'll never want to come. Her husband earns a fortune with some City bank. She'll want to be where ever he is.' This assumption is not only inherently sexist, it's also rather risky: it might well be that Mary's husband is only too happy to follow Mary, particularly if he's always fancied selling up and running a smallholding in the country.

In short, when it comes to everyday gossip around the office, managers cannot assume that employees either say what they mean or mean what they say, even about the simplest subjects. Casual chatter, over morning coffee or in the pub, cannot be used as the basis for significant management actions. If managers want to make reliable and appropriate decisions, they must make conscious, active and systematic efforts to find out what their employees *really* think.

Stirring up trouble?

This is all very well, you may say, but it doesn't overcome the third problem mentioned above: managers are reluctant to seek their employees' views because it can only stir up trouble. Well, there's certainly some justice in this view: a survey *is* very likely to influence the overall attitudes of the workforce. It raises expectations of some management response. It highlights issues that may previously have been hidden or unacknowledged. It encourages employees to discuss ideas and share experiences. In other words, to misapply Heisenberg's Uncertainty Principle, the act of observing is bound to affect what is observed. The simple process of eliciting employees' opinions, even if no further action is taken, is likely to change the situation. Indeed, if no further action *is* taken, it will very probably change the situation for the worse.

This is certainly an important issue, which we'll be examining much more closely later on. However, it's not necessarily a problem, and it shouldn't discourage managers from seeking employee views. After all, if the process arouses significant discontent, it's very likely that this discontent would have arisen anyway, in some form and at some place. More important, it would have been festering away for a longer period before emerging, with no official means of finding expression. When it did finally emerge, it would probably be even more destructive, with its causes unclear and no immediate mechanism for resolving it. If employees cannot express concerns about pay or working conditions in any other way, they will probably end up voting with their feet. This may take the form of industrial action or, more commonly, just low motivation, high absenteeism and increasing staff turnover. In the latter case, managers may not even realize they have a problem until it reaches epidemic proportions.

On the other hand, if the discontent emerges through a management-inspired process of consultation, management at least has the initiative. The problem may be difficult to resolve, but managers know a problem exists and have some insight into its causes. Management might even gain a few brownie points for raising the issue in the first place. In the harsh world of employee relations, every little helps.

Still, there's no doubt that employee consultation, however conducted, is often the tin opener to a huge can of worms. Even if no major problems emerge, the process itself will set up certain expectations, which demand management action. Many of the managers involved will end up wondering why on earth they started it all in the first place. The whole exercise will be highly demanding and will probably bring a fair few headaches before it begins to bring results.

But this is not an argument for not doing it – quite the reverse. It's merely an argument for ensuring that it is done effectively, with the minimum of pain and the maximum of results.

So what should you do?

This book arises from three simple (though not necessarily comfortable) premises, namely that:

- It's becoming increasingly important for managers to base their decisions and actions on an accurate understanding of what their employees *really* think, feel and desire
- This understanding is most effectively gained through a systematic, formal and confidential process
- The process is likely to be difficult, demanding and to require a high level of commitment from the managers involved.

Subsequent chapters aim to provide managers with an understanding of the likely relevance and value of employee surveys for their organizations. Second, they offer a straightforward, jargon-free account of the approaches, tools and techniques that can be used in preparing for and conducting the survey. Third, and perhaps most important, they outline what should happen once the survey is complete. All too often managers assume that, once they have gathered their employees' views, they can sit back and relax. In reality, that's where the hard work really starts. If the survey isn't followed by management action – or if the action is inappropriate – the whole exercise will have been at best a waste of everyone's time. More likely, as in the example quoted earlier, it will have caused even more problems.

The book is aimed at the growing band of managers who are developing an interest in the area of employee surveys, and are perhaps considering conducting a survey in their own organizations. This may be in response to particular concerns, such as high staff turnover or absenteeism, poor industrial relations or low productivity. It may be as a preliminary to some specific management initiative, such as relocation, restructuring or a change in reward strategy. It may even be simply because the manager feels it would be helpful to gain a greater understanding of employee attitudes or opinions.

Employee surveys can be valuable in all these circumstances, provided that sufficient thought and effort are put into all stages of the survey process, from the initial preparation through to the implementation of an action plan based on the findings. The following chapters guide the reader through the minefield of the survey process, identifying the key issues and likely problems at each stage. Above all, the book concentrates on the *practicalities* of conducting surveys in an employment context. And, while success cannot be guaranteed, this should at least help managers put their ears to the ground without fear of passing stagecoaches!

Chapter One

Why Do We Need to Survey Our Employees, Anyway?

'. . . the deep
Moans round with many voices. Come, my friends,
'Tis not too late to seek a newer world'

Tennyson, 'Ulysses'

A colleague of mine was recently asked by the Regional Personnel Manager of a well-known company to conduct a survey of its employees. 'Fine,' she said. 'Only too happy to oblige. Now, why do you want the survey exactly?'

The Personnel Manager shuffled his papers embarrassedly. 'Oh well, you know. We think it's a good idea. Lots of people are doing them, aren't they? Participative management and all that.'

'Yes, indeed,' said my colleague. 'But why do you want to conduct one now, particularly?'

'Well, you know,' said the Personnel Manager, shuffling his papers some more. 'Always a good idea to find out what everyone thinks. Get everyone's views. That kind of thing.'

'Yes, indeed,' replied by colleague, patiently, sensing a potentially lucrative assignment evaporating before her eyes. She decided to try another tack. 'So, what do you want to find out? What kind of subjects do you want the survey to cover?'

'Subjects?' asked the Personnel Manager, looking slightly startled. 'Well, I don't know, exactly. I thought we'd leave that up to you. I mean, you're the experts. What do surveys normally cover?'

'Well, it depends,' said my colleague, deciding that patience is

8

definitely a virtue, if not necessarily an easy one. 'Some look at the employees' overall levels of satisfaction with the employer or with their work. Some look at management style or corporate culture. Some look at specifics, like the payment system or working methods. Some get right down to basics, looking at things like the working environment or even the staff restaurant . . . '

'Yes, yes,' interrupted the Personnel Manager. 'That sounds about right. It could cover all those things.'

At this point, my colleague's patience finally began to wear a little thin, and she asked the Personnel Manager exactly where the idea of a survey had come from. The Personnel Manager hesitated and blushed slightly. Then he admitted that the idea hadn't been his, but had been devolved by his boss, the Personnel Director. 'Perhaps,' my colleague suggested, 'we should talk to him and see what he had in mind?'

After some further hesitation the Personnel Manager agreed and a meeting with the Personnel Director was arranged. To my colleague's dismay, the Personnel Director's response to her questions was identical to that of his subordinate. So, finally, as before, she asked the Personnel Director where the idea had come from. 'Well, actually,' he admitted, 'it wasn't my idea. It was the MD's. He put it in my annual objectives. I think he'd read an article about employee surveys in the *Economist* . . . '

As this story indicates, organizations decide to conduct surveys for a variety of reasons, some better than others. Very often, as in this case, the initial motivation is little more than a senior management whim. After all, communication is a good thing. And you can't have too much of a good thing, can you? Unfortunately, in this case, you certainly can, especially if no thought's been given to the purpose of the whole exercise in the first place.

At the opposite extreme, many organizations go for years on end with no evident interest in what their employees think about anything. Business strategies change, old markets contract and new ones develop, directors come and go, working practices alter, new remuneration systems are introduced, and the organization never thinks to ask *employees* what they think about any of this. 'Oh, we don't need to,' managers say. 'They're all happy enough. Anyway, if they're not, they don't have to work here.' The organization continues to prosper – more or less. It continues to grow

– though not as quickly as in its heyday. It makes a profit – though that's been down for the last couple of years.

So why worry?

Many organizations really begin to worry about what their employees think only when a serious problem arises. Most commonly, and most dramatically, it is an industrial-relations problem. After the umpteenth change in employment practices, the previously docile local branch of the trade union decides that enough is enough. Suddenly, management finds itself facing industrial action for the first time in living memory. And, of course, feelings on both sides are now running so high that compromise is impossible, even though the immediate cause of the dispute may be quite trivial. There have been numerous major disputes in recent years which can be seen, at least in part, as manifestations of deep-rooted discontents. The recent industrial action taken by, for example, ambulance workers or teachers arguably stemmed as much from long-term dissatisfaction with treatment of the health service or education as from immediate pay demands. All too often, the apparent cause of industrial unrest is little more than the final straw.

Of course, employee discontent does not always find expression in industrial action. Indeed, for many employees – such as those who work in non-unionized environments or lack effective bargaining power – industrial action may not be a viable option. But this doesn't mean that no problem exists. In some cases, employees may indeed have decided, in the words of the hypothetical manager quoted above, that they 'don't have to work here'. It may well take managers some time to realize that they have a problem. After all, high staff turnover for a short period or in one or two departments may be just coincidental.

Is employee turnover a problem?

Even if managers do spot that turnover is rising, they often just assume that their salaries are becoming uncompetitive. When asked if they have difficulty recruiting staff, they respond, 'No, we don't usually have too much of a problem recruiting the right kind of people, but we have the Devil's own job persuading them to stay for more than a year or so . . . ' Well, it's possible that the salary is uncompetitive, but in that case why are employees willing to come in the first place? It's more likely that there are other problems – lack of career opportunities, dissatisfaction with the overall organizational culture, insufficient job satisfaction, or any of the myriad reasons that make people decide to change jobs.

Even if management does eventually realize that high turnover is a problem, it's usually much more difficult to root out the underlying causes. Exit interviews may help to provide information about employees' reasons for leaving, but even these can be misleading. After all, it's uncommon for an employee to accept a lower salary or fewer career-development opportunities when changing jobs, so exit interview notes tend to be full of anodyne phrases like 'Leaving for better pay' or 'Looking for career change'. All too often, these fail to add the all-important qualifying clause that goes something like ' . . . but I wouldn't have been looking for another job if the working conditions here weren't so awful' or ' . . . but I only want to change careers because I'm sick of working in such an authoritarian culture'.

To illustrate this, consider the experience of one UK company which was having major difficulties in retaining its graduate trainees. As an initial response to this problem, the company had given several disproportionate increases to graduate salaries. The company attracted greater and greater numbers of new graduates through the milk round, and felt that it was recruiting higher-quality applicants. But retention didn't improve – in fact, it became even worse. Moreover, resentment was growing among non-graduate staff, who saw inexperienced graduates being paid higher salaries. This in turn had a knock-on effect on morale and performance among the rest of the company.

Eventually, when the problem was reaching crisis level, the company conducted a survey to find out the real reasons why graduates were not staying. The response – from graduates and non-graduates alike – was virtually unanimous. The company recruited very highly qualified graduates, many with first-class degrees or postgraduate qualifications. However, because of the graduates' lack of experience, the company could only offer comparatively mundane work. Indeed, many graduates felt that they were given tasks which had been artificially created to 'give them something to do'. There were few opportunities to move into 'real' jobs for several years and the initial high salary meant that subsequent salary increases tended not to reflect the individual's progress.

Above all, most felt that the company's bureaucratic management structure conflicted strongly with the image given in its glossy recruitment literature, which promised 'challenging, demanding responsibility'. As a result, within a year or two, most graduate trainees, despite being better paid than many of their contemporaries, began to get itchy feet and left. In short, the survey revealed that the company misunderstood the cause of the problem. As a result, its instinctive response to put things right – increasing graduate salaries – was actually making matters worse!

Other signs of discontent

High staff turnover is one of the more obvious expressions of employee discontent. Other manifestations may be harder to spot. For instance, if there are few other job opportunities in the area, turnover may remain low, even though the workforce is highly dissatisfied. Discontent may then only be expressed through low morale, poor motivation and, as a result, declining productivity or service.

In a manufacturing or production industry, low productivity should eventually be apparent, though it may still take a lot of management effort to discover that the cause is employee discontent, rather than faults in production methods or working arrangements. In a service industry, declining standards may be much harder to spot, at least until they begin to have an effect on profits. Even then, there may be a hundred reasons why profits have declined – economic conditions, competitor pressure, changes in the marketplace. It will probably take managers a long time, working against the clock of liquidation or bankruptcy, before they realize that their major problems lie in the poor service given by their staff. And it may take even longer before they understand the specific causes of this poor service. By that time, even if they do understand the real problem, it will probably be too late to begin the painful process of trying to put things right.

A company on the brink of bankruptcy is not likely to be too concerned about whether its employees are happy in their work. It's possible that the sense of crisis, perhaps coupled with the dismissal of the entire senior management team, will encourage improvements in individual and company performance. If it does, this may be enough to save the company, but it may well leave the root problems unresolved. Once the company begins to get back on an even keel, the same old dissatisfactions recur and the vicious circle starts all over again. The reader probably won't have to think too hard to come up with a number of well-known companies which have walked this nerve-wracking line between survival and disaster in recent years.

Do we really have a problem?

Ideally, then, employers need to begin to tackle the causes of employee discontent long before they reach crisis point or begin to have a noticeable effect on the bottom line. However, this presents a problem. If the feelings of the employees are not yet significantly affecting performance or productivity, and if there are no obvious manifestations of discontent, how does the employer know when there's a problem? How does the employer go about investigating employee attitudes or views, unless it's clear that there's something worth investigating?

As the anecdote at the start of this chapter indicates, it's not usually possible or desirable for the employer just to dig around randomly in the hope of striking some cause for concern. Employee surveys can cover a wide spectrum of subject matter, from abstract issues about corporate culture or company values through to very concrete issues, like the standard of food in the staff canteen. No survey could cover all these issues, except so superficially that the results would be meaningless. 'Are you generally happy with the culture of the company?' would probably be unanswerable in less than 5,000 words. 'Are you generally happy with the standard of food in the staff canteen?' might be slightly easier, but not much. As we'll see when we come to look at issues of questionnaire design, it's essential that respondents are asked questions which are both precise and answerable, which leave little room for ambiguity and which can be used to provide meaningful comparisons across the sample.

If these requirements are to be fulfilled, it's likely that the overall questionnaire will only be able to cover a very limited range of subject matter. Even with a comparatively straightforward issue such as the staff canteen, a fairly long and detailed questionnaire would be needed to cover usefully all possible areas of concern. At the same time, if the survey is to provide the basis for subsequent management action, it must cover all significant factors. A survey on the canteen might cover the quality of the food in detail, but make no mention of the standard of service. As a result, management might end up spending large sums of money responding to comparatively minor quibbles about the food, but be totally unaware of a much greater dissatisfaction with the way the food is served or the canteen organized.

Focussing the survey

This brings us, right at the start, up against the central paradox of employee surveys – and indeed of surveys in general. It's very difficult to carry out a survey unless you already have a good idea of what you are trying to find out. In an ideal world, it might be possible to carry out a series of successive surveys, each more precise than the last. The first might be very broad, simply to highlight general areas of concern. The second would be more precise, focussing on the areas highlighted by the first survey, investigating the particular aspects which need to be addressed. And so on. Eventually, the surveyors would probably be able to develop a perfect questionnaire which would ask, precisely and appropriately, all the questions that were relevant. Management could then act on the results and all would be right with the world.

In practice, few employers would be prepared to devote such resources to investigating their employees' views, just on the off chance that some problem might emerge. It would be a very costly way of discovering that your employees are all pretty content, by and large, thank you very much. More importantly, as we mentioned in the Introduction, there's no doubt that the very act of surveying would itself influence attitudes.

Conducting regular surveys

Some organizations have tried to get round this problem by instituting regular employee surveys, perhaps carried out annually or every couple of years. This has become fairly common practice, for example, in some of the larger 'blue chip' organizations, which have a comparatively high level of resources to devote to such exercises. These regular surveys generally resemble the first in the sequence described above. Their scope is usually very broad, skimming across a range of areas where problems might have arisen: general job satisfaction, career development, pay, management style, overall corporate culture, and so on. The aim would be simply to highlight apparent problems, rather than to explore them in detail. If there appeared to be problems in a particular area, then further investigations – including a more detailed survey – could be carried out, to probe deeper.

This kind of regular survey brings a number of benefits. First, it enables the employer to spot possible problems at an early opportunity, before they're apparent to the naked eye. Second, because the survey is held regularly, employees grow accustomed to the process. They have fewer worries about participating and fewer expectations that management action will automatically follow. Third, and perhaps most important of all, the repetition of the survey provides comparative benchmarks against which results can be judged. As we'll see later, it is often difficult to decide what the results of employee surveys actually *mean*. If the survey indicates that 30% of your workforce is dissatisfied with pay, is that acceptable or not? Is it a good result or a bad one? In isolation, it's often difficult to answer these questions. There's no absolute answer, and even comparisons with other organizations can be misleading. After all, the result may be affected by a host of factors – the state of the local labour market, the nature of the work, the expectations of the workforce, the history of the organization. Quite often, the most useful comparisons will be internal. If the level of dissatisfaction is significantly higher in Department A than in Department B, then it's possible to investigate the likely causes. Similarly, if the workforce has been asked the same or similar questions repeatedly over a period of some years, it'll be possible to spot apparent trends or changes in response. If the proportion of the workforce expressing concern about pay suddenly increases, then it is possible to investigate the reasons for the increase.

A regular overview survey can be a valuable barometer – or perhaps seismometer – of employee opinion, highlighting areas of potential concern and providing the basis for more detailed investigation and action. However, as we'll see, surveying is usually fairly costly, and many organizations would probably have difficulty justifying the expense on a regular basis. Most employers, if they consider surveying at all, still think of it as a 'one-off' process, undertaken in response to some particular need.

Furthermore, although regular surveying can be highly beneficial, it's not fool-proof, and the results can be misleading. No matter how wide the scope of the survey, it will almost certainly miss some potentially significant areas. It's not unusual for dissatisfaction to arise about some comparatively peripheral issue – the state of office accommodation or some particular work practice, for instance. General questions about overall job satisfaction or company culture might well fail to unearth these more specific concerns. As a result, management assumes that everything is fine until the discontent begins to spill over into other areas or until employees begin to express a more general discontent. By that stage, the problem may have gained an unwarranted momentum. Worse still, management may have become so complacent that they fail to recognize the signs of discontent until it's too late.

Similarly, although regular surveys can provide valuable advance warning of problems, they may distract attention from other warning signs. If the survey is only carried out annually or even less frequently, it is quite possible that problems will arise between surveys. By the time the next survey comes around, the problem can have grown significantly. Again, if management have been enticed into complacency by the survey results, they may decide to ignore other, less formal signs of discontent. It is all too easy to imagine a manager saying to his shop steward, 'Don't be daft. I know you've had a few complaints about such and such, but they're just from one or two moaning minnies. They're not representative. Look, the survey results prove it!'

So, even if you can afford to run regular diagnostic surveys, these probably won't solve all your problems. In that case, you may well ask, how can employers be sure of identifying issues of potential concern or which may require more thorough investigation? How can managers spot when a detailed survey might be helpful?

Identifying the problems

There's no single mechanism, no matter how costly or sophisticated, which will unerringly warn managers that trouble is brewing or that action needs to be taken. The only effective approach is to make use of a range of different approaches, pay attention to a range of potentially significant indices and, above all, *keep your eyes and ears open.*

If you can afford to conduct an annual diagnostic survey, by all means do so. But don't assume that you then need to take no further action. If you can't afford to conduct an annual survey, don't despair; there are plenty of other useful approaches.

First of all, and perhaps most importantly, managers should pay close attention to a range of *statistical indices*. If interpreted thoughtfully, these can give a powerful insight into potential or actual employment problems. Some of these indices we've already mentioned in passing. They include staff turnover and wastage, levels of absenteeism, productivity levels (where these exist and are relevant), recruitment statistics, and so on.

For those who are not already producing and analysing statistics in these areas, there is a wealth of available literature explaining how this can be done. I don't propose to go into the mechanics of these indices in depth, but readers who are interested in pursuing these issues can consult some of the books recommended in the Bibliography. Many are very good at explaining the technicalities of data collection and analysis. They are often less good at providing practical guidance on what managers should do with the results. And this is not always as obvious as it appears. It's perhaps helpful, therefore, briefly to consider some of the possible implications of these indices, and how they should be followed up. As an illustration, let's start by looking in some detail at one of the indices we've already mentioned.

Employee turnover

This can be defined as the number of employees leaving the
organization, for whatever reason, over a given period. It is one
of the most basic elements of human-resource information. In
most organizations, particularly in these days of computerization,
it should be straightforward to collect and analyse. Efforts should
be made to ensure that relevant turnover information is made
available to *all* managers, both line and personnel. All too often,
turnover data is only provided to personnel staff and a small
number of senior managers (who probably don't have time to
look at it anyway, unless some major problem or trend is brought
to their attention).

In the first place, personnel departments need access to *organiz-
ation-wide turnover data*. They are usually the only people who
are in a position to identify and analyse trends across all departments and functions. At the same time, however much personnel
staff may have their fingers on the pulse of the organization, they
may still fail to understand the full significance of such information. For example, if turnover in a given department has suddenly increased over a particular period, the personnel department may be unaware of the cause unless they investigate the
matter with the line manager involved. If the increase is only a
comparatively minor one, they may even fail to notice it or feel
that it is not worth exploring further. On the other hand, the line
manager, who understands the department's working practices
and operational pressures, may think to relate the increase to
a specific cause, such as the heightened stress accompanying a
particular piece of work or time of year.

The message is clear. Turnover information – and the whole
range of similar statistics – should be provided, in appropriate
form and detail, to *all* relevant managers. Furthermore, though
this may prove the difficult bit, managers should be encouraged
to read and make use of such data. This probably means that the
statistics need to be presented in a concise, ready-prepared and
easily digested form. There's no point in expecting a busy Production Manager to plough through page after page of closely
packed computer printout in the hope of stumbling across some
nugget of information that might be relevant. The raw data needs
to be carefully processed and the relevant indices prepared – we'll

consider what these are in more detail in a moment. They should be set out in a clear and comprehensible form, and any apparent trends or highlights should be identified. The less work managers have to do in studying the statistics, the more likely they are to come up with helpful and illuminating comments. The whole process may be a bit of a chore – and unfortunately personnel is probably the most appropriate function to take it on – but it may well lead to some surprising and valuable results.

Preparing the data

So, how should wastage information be analysed, and what indices should be included? In practice, this will probably depend on a number of factors, including the nature of the organization, overall expectations about likely problem areas or issues and the amount of time and resources available. Managers will need to make their own judgements about how much detail is needed and what level of resources can be justified.

In broad terms, employee wastage is normally divided in two kinds: *voluntary* and *involuntary*. Involuntary wastage includes employees who cease working for the organization because of dismissal, retirement, redundancy and, of course, death. Voluntary wastage covers all those employees who resign from the organization of their own free will, for whatever reason. Clearly, for the purposes of identifying potential problems or areas that require more systematic investigation, the latter group is likely to be the more illuminating. An abnormally high level of voluntary wastage, either in a given department or over a given period, may well indicate some problem worthy of investigation. Equally, a rising trend may reflect some discontent or concern which can be explored further.

Statistics for involuntary wastage are likely to be less helpful. After all, the organization should already be aware of the reasons for dismissal or redundancy, and death is not normally indicative of attitudes to work. Moreover, during normal times, involuntary departures are likely to be an extremely small proportion of the overall wastage figures.

Nonetheless, statistics for involuntary wastage shouldn't be disregarded entirely. Occasionally, they may reflect some significant trend or issue. For example, an above average number of dismissals for poor performance over a given period might possibly carry wider implications in terms of motivation, working practices, management style or employer expectations. In other words, the dismissals may be merely the most extreme manifestation of a more widespread problem.

Redundancy is unlikely to indicate much about the attitudes of those being made redundant – except in those cases where redundancy is simply a polite euphemism for sacking. However, it may well indicate something about the attitudes of other employees. A single redundancy in a given department – especially if badly handled or perceived as unfair – may have a severely detrimental effect on morale and attitudes. If there has been a redundancy, no matter how reasonable and justified from management's perspective, it may well be a good idea to keep a watchful eye for other signs of trouble.

Even death may sometimes indicate wider problems. Generally speaking, death is no more than, as it were, an unfortunate fact of life. If an employee gets run over by a bus or contracts some terminal disease, this is no reflection on the organization he or she happens to work for. Nevertheless, if there are an unexpectedly high number of untimely deaths, particularly when these appear to be partly stress-related, this might be a reflection on management attitudes or working practices. One or two heart attacks or strokes over a period might be coincidence. A larger number might begin to suggest carelessness, and could indicate an area worthy of further investigation.

Turnover indices

Apart from this straightforward division between voluntary and involuntary wastage, labour turnover can be analysed in many ways and degrees of detail. The most appropriate form of turnover analysis is usually what's sometimes called the *central wastage rate*, given by the following formula:

$$\frac{\text{Number of leavers from a particular group during a given period}}{\text{Average number in the group during that period}}$$

Multiplied by 100, this formula will give the labour turnover as a percentage. Clearly, the group analysed and the period chosen will depend on the organization's particular needs. The most straightforward analysis would be the number of employees leaving the whole organization during a year, which would give the *annual labour turnover*. For example, if 40 employees left an organization with an average size of 1,000 employees during the year, this would give a labour turnover of 4%.

What's an acceptable level of turnover?

In isolation, the turnover rate is fairly meaningless. Is 4% good or bad? Is there cause for concern? In fact, most organizations tend to assume that a certain element of turnover is probably inevitable and even desirable. After all, if no one leaves and the organization isn't growing significantly, it may be very difficult to bring in new blood and new ideas. Most organizations tend to assume that turnover up to around 10% or perhaps even higher is acceptable. But this will depend very much on the nature and circumstances of the organization. For example, if the organization is endeavouring to provide the highest pay and best working conditions in its field, it would probably expect a correspondingly low level of staff turnover. The same might be true of an organization in an area of very high unemployment. In these cases, a turnover figure of even 5% might be a cause for concern. At the opposite extreme, an organization might decide to pay comparatively low salary levels and accept a correspondingly high labour turnover. In the latter case, the organization might be willing to accept 20% or even higher, and only really begin to worry once turnover creeps above 30%.

In short, there's no absolute answer to the question: 'What's an acceptable level of turnover?' For most organizations, the mose useful answers will be comparative. Several possible sources of comparison are available. Managers can try to obtain comparative figures from other organizations in the same geographical area and industrial sector. If every other employer in the town has a turnover of 8% whereas yours is 15%, then you may well have cause for concern. In practice, reliable figures are notoriously hard to get hold of. After all, most employers will be fairly reluctant to admit publicly to high labour turnover, as this won't do a lot to improve their future ability to recruit good-quality employees. However, there are one or two sources of published information – usually anonymous and aggregated – and you may also be able to get hold of more detailed information on a reciprocal basis through contacts in other companies.

In any case, this is not the only source of comparisons. In many cases, the most useful comparisons may be internal ones. Assuming that records are available (and if they're not, at least you can make sure they are from now on), you can analyse employee turnover by department or function and over several years.

Turnover in particular groups

It's also possible to carry out a *cohort analysis* of employee wastage – that is, the wastage of a predetermined cohort or group of employees over a period of years. This can be particularly helpful in investigating problems among a specific group. For example, if, as in the example given earlier, there's concern about turnover among graduate trainees, the analyst might take the cohort of trainees which joined in a given year – say, five years earlier – and examine their wastage up to the present day. This can be very revealing. The results for a group of 30 graduates might be as follows:

During 1st year	–	Numbers departing: 1
During 2nd year	–	Numbers departing: 3
During 3rd year	–	Numbers departing: 7
During 4th year	–	Numbers departing: 18
During 5th year	–	Numbers departing: 2

In this case, there's an apparent problem in the fourth year, when turnover increases dramatically. This might be coincidence, but it may well be possible to identify some specific cause. Perhaps trainees receive high levels of annual pay increase during the first three years, after which salary increases become much more modest. Perhaps fourth-year trainees have to compete for promotion or non-trainee posts for the first time. If so, trainees may feel that they might as well compete in the external labour market instead.

It's also worth noting that, after the fourth year, turnover drops considerably. This may just indicate that the most marketable trainees have left. More optimistically, it may indicate that trainees tend to stay with the organization, once they've passed the fourth-year hurdle. Again, these kinds of hypotheses can be investigated through more detailed surveys. The organization can then make appropriate changes in its employment or recruitment practices.

To illustrate how this might work in practice, let's look at a specific example. One company in my experience, having identified this kind of turnover pattern among its graduate trainees, conducted a survey amongst a sample to discover the reasons. To the company's surprise, the survey indicated that discontent stemmed not from concerns about work or pay, but quite simply from *restlessness*. The company tended to recruit highly qualified and marketable graduates, who often felt reluctant to spend the rest of their careers in the same organization, however good the conditions and prospects. As a result, a large proportion of trainees left during the first two or three years. On the other hand, those who stayed beyond four or five years tended to remain with the company for many years.

On the basis of this insight, the company altered its recruitment policy, making conscious efforts to identify candidates who would want to make a long-term career with the company. In particular, it began to recruit older candidates, who had already gained some work experience and who were often willing to commit themselves to the company on a more permanent basis. Within a few years, graduate turnover was significantly reduced.

Absenteeism

Another valuable indicator of actual or potential problems is *absenteeism*. As with labour turnover, absence rates can be analysed and presented in a variety of ways, depending on the information available and the needs of the organization. However, the simplest and probably most useful formula is:

Number of working hours/days lost in a period
Number of possible working hours/days in the period.

Multiplied by 100, this gives the *absence rate* as a percentage.
As with turnover, the analysis can be carried out for the whole
organization or for specific departments. Comparisons can be
made with other organizations (though, again, these are not
always easy to get hold of), with published figures, between
departments or functions, and over time. By making relevant
comparisons it should be possible to highlight trends or unexpected changes, and these in their turn may indicate areas worthy of
further investigation.

For example, if absence appears high in a particular department, you might investigate attitudes to the department's working
methods or the style of its manager. If absence increases during
a particular period, you might link this to a hypothetical cause.
You might, for example, find that absence is highest during (or
shortly after) quarter- or year-end periods, when the workload is
heaviest. This could lead you to investigate employee feelings
about their workloads, levels of responsibility or overall stress.
Alternatively, you might find that absence is highest during good
weather or when there's a Test Match on television. This could
lead you to ask employees some questions about motivation or
commitment!

Performance and productivity

Absence analysis, like labour-turnover analysis, can be carried
out in virtually any employing organization. Other indicators are
likely to be more specific to particular industries or types of organization. For example, in a manufacturing company productivity
would be a key index. Similarly, retail organizations usually analyse performance on the basis of sales per unit of floor area or
some similar formula. Indices of this kind can clearly be invaluable
indicators of potential or actual problems. However, many managers are still much more accustomed to using such indices as
straightforward guides to performance than as signposts for further investigation. If production in a given area is unsatisfactory,
the manager simply assumes that this is due to poor individual

performance. A little bit of exhortation, a few strong words to the slackers, and the problem should sort itself out. And if that doesn't work, perhaps we need more capital investment. Or different working methods. Or . . .

The truth is that poor performance, whether corporate, departmental or individual, may well be indicative of some more deep-seated problem. At a personal level, it may stem from domestic difficulties, illness or a range of other causes. At a corporate or departmental level, it may stem from problems with working methods, dissatisfaction with management style, general low morale, or many other factors. As with turnover and absence, productivity or performance indices do not generally provide an answer in themselves. Rather, they are symptoms of matters which need to be examined in more detail. They need to be considered thoughtfully and in context. Is productivity in Department A higher than productivity in Department B? Have sales in Store X suddenly dipped whereas those in other stores have remained constant or improved? If so, can these changes be hypothetically linked to any internal or external factors? Was a new manager appointed? Have working methods changed? Rather than taking the statistics at face value, managers should take account of all relevant factors in making tentative judgements about possible causes or implications. These judgements can then be used as the basis for more formal investigation.

Other signs of trouble

In most organizations, there are countless other statistics which can be used in this way, each of which may help to clarify the overall picture. In a retail or service organization, it may be relevant to consider the numbers and types of comments or complaints received from customers. A high level of complaints is clearly a cause of concern. More important, particular kinds of complaint might shed light on other statistics. If there are repeated comments about staff apparently having insufficient time to serve customers or being unable to deal effectively with a wide range of responsibilities, this could well shed light on reasons for high turnover or absenteeism.

Other relevant statistics might include recruitment or job application statistics. If advertisements consistently attract low numbers of suitable applicants, even though salaries appear to be competitive, this might indicate something about perceptions of the organization among the workforce as well as the community at large. In organizations where the staff are expected to compete for internal vacancies, job application figures can be even more revealing. If a particular department continually attracts comparatively low numbers of applicants or if unexpectedly low numbers apply for particular promotions, this might indicate factors worthy of further investigation.

Watching and listening

Of course, these kinds of formal statistical indices are only part of the picture. Astute managers will also keep their eyes and ears open for less formal indicators of problems or issues which merit closer examination. Earlier, we warned about the dangers of paying too close attention to coffee-time gossip. Nonetheless, if taken with appropriate shovelfuls of salt, such gossip can provide valuable signposts. The gossip may be exaggerated and the gossipers may have misinterpreted events, but the simple fact that people are talking suggests that there is *something* worth talking about.

It's all too easy for the busy manager to dismiss office gossip or moans, particularly if the content is inaccurate or trivial. But, like the more formal indices discussed above, such responses may often be indicative of more substantial discontents. One of my earliest experiences as a personnel practitioner was dealing with repeated complaints from junior clerical and finance staff about the quality of the air conditioning in their part of the building. We *knew* there was nothing wrong with the air conditioning. There were no complaints from anywhere else in the building. The complaints weren't consistent – some felt it was too hot, some too cold and some just too airless. We'd had the engineers in a dozen times to look at it and they could find nothing wrong, and certainly nothing different from anywhere else in the building. We'd spent days working up there ourselves, listening to people saying, 'See, it's far too hot' or 'Well, I bet you're cold too now you're up here' or 'You've got to agree that you can't expect people to work in this kind of airless environment.'

Despite our reassurances, the complaints went on. Eventually, not entirely by coincidence, we decided to reorganize the distribution of staff around the building. We moved all the clerical and finance staff to the other end of the site, into a different building, and we replaced them with a group of professional computer programmers and systems designers. As we expected, complaints about the former problem area ceased. The new residents, when asked about the air conditioning, said, with puzzled expressions, 'It's fine. Seems the same as where we were before. Why do you ask?' But, you won't be surprised to hear, a new rash of complaints had now sprung up, this time about the building where we'd moved the finance and clerical staff . . .

The point about this story is that, in itself, the complaint was trivial and almost certainly inaccurate. However, it was a symptom of a more deep-rooted problem which – once we'd decided to stop summoning the air-conditioning engineers – we were able to investigate by surveying employee opinion. Readers won't be surprised to learn that dissatisfaction with the working environment reflected dissatisfaction with the routine nature of the work. In some cases, employees were consciously raising complaints both as a protest and as a means of alleviating their boredom. In other cases, with time and mental energy on their hands, employees were simply focussing on comparatively minor issues which would otherwise have gone unnoticed.

It's worth remembering that, if employees lack formal mechanisms to voice their feelings of discontent, they will tend to express their protests through whatever channels *are* available. If the organization encourages employees to make comments about canteen food or there's a consultative body to discuss aspects of the work environment, there'll probably be a high level of complaints in these areas. Care needs to be taken in this respect, as we shall see, even when conducting more formal surveys of employee opinion. If management decides to conduct a survey about relocation while the employees are still aggrieved about an unsatisfactory pay deal, they may well take the opportunity to express their anger, even if this distorts their responses to the subject at hand.

Similarly, if employees are unable to express their feelings through official channels, they may well find unofficial ways. We have already talked about employee turnover, absenteeism and low productivity, the most straightforward forms of protest. But it's not unknown for employees also to introduce minor forms of sabotage: temporarily stopping machines, fouling up administrative or management systems, nit-picking about demarcation or job descriptions. Like the complaints about air conditioning, these actions are both a protest and a means of alleviating boredom. Once again, managers need to pay attention to such phenomena – high incidence of machine or hardware breakdown, an unexpected number of errors from an experienced operator, or whatever. As with low productivity, the first reaction of many managers is to take some form of disciplinary action. In the longer term, this might be appropriate. But before taking any precipitate steps, managers should ask themselves *why* employees are behaving in this way. Does their action, however trivial and mindless it appears, reflect some more significant concern? If so, steps should be taken to understand this concern and, if possible, to put it right.

Proactive surveys

Up until now in this chapter, we've looked at the various indicators that managers might use to obtain an early warning of potential problems. Our assumption has been that organizations will generally want to carry out surveys in response to actual or potential difficulties, so that the survey can be used as a basis for understanding the problem and devising an appropriate remedy. In general, this is likely to be the most common use of surveys. After all, as we have already indicated, surveying is usually difficult, traumatic and costly. Most organizations will be reluctant to embark on this process except in response to some significant problem.

Nevertheless, the process does not have to be quite so reactive and pessimistic. There will certainly be occasions when organizations wish to initiate surveys for their own purposes. You might, for example, conduct a survey prior to the introduction of new working practices or a new remuneration system. You might wish to gain an understanding of employees' likes and dislikes about the current systems, so that the new design can take these into account. On the other hand, you might conduct a survey *after* the new system has been introduced. In this case, the aim would be to gather employee responses to the new system, so that it can be altered or fine-tuned.

Surveys can also be used to assess employee attitudes and opinions before or after a major organizational or corporate change. It's common for companies to initiate surveys after acquisitions or mergers, so that possible problems and areas of strength can be identified as soon as possible. In the public sector, surveys have often been used by bodies undergoing some form of privatization.

In addition, surveys can be used, sometimes on a continuing basis, to assess the success of a particular management initiative. For example, if the organization has introduced a Total Quality initiative or a major culture-change exercise, employee surveys can be used to assess how effective the process has been and how far down the hierarchy the changes have penetrated. A survey might indicate, for example, that while 'quality' is the paramount objective for senior managers, it is still much less important than productivity or even personal convenience for junior employees.

Summary

- Employee surveys *can* be used as crisis measures, but it is far better to try and spot potential problems at an earlier stage
- Identify the specific issues which require investigation in advance – successful surveys need a sharp focus
- Day-to-day problems in industrial relations, for example, are often merely symptoms of far deeper causes
- Statistics for employee turnover, absenteeism, performance and productivity can all give early signs that further investigation is needed
- Only very large organizations can afford the expense of regular employee surveys
- Proactive surveys are often appropriate before or after relocation or major organizational changes in working methods

- Comparative data (i.e. between departments or overtime) is often far more useful than raw figures
- Keep your ears and eyes open – there are many clues to employees' dissatisfactions and anxieties.

Chapter Two

What is an Employee Survey?

*'All the business of war, and indeed all the business of life, is to endeavour
to find out what you don't know by what you do; that's what I called
"guessing what was at the other side of the hill"'*

Duke of Wellington, Croker Papers

In the previous chapter, we examined some of the indicators that
might prompt managers to carry out more detailed and formal
investigations of employee opinions. But we haven't yet really
defined what sort of process we're really talking about. Before
we proceed any further, let's take some time to consider what we
mean by an 'employee survey' and what kinds of tools are likely
to be helpful in conducting such a survey.

First of all, to clarify one point, readers will notice that so far
there's been no use of the more familiar term *attitude survey*. This
is deliberate. Although the term is widely used to describe a whole
range of survey instruments, many people still see them as rather
mysterious processes designed to uncover employees' most secret
thoughts. Some even regard them as a form of black magic,
practised only by initiates and threatening in their intent.

This kind of perception does nobody any good. It means that
managers are nervous of using surveys unless they hand the whole
process over to 'experts'. It means that, even when the experts
have completed their work, managers are not sufficiently involved
to make good practical use of the results. And, above all, it means
that employees view the whole exercise as a threat. This may in
turn mean that they are reluctant to co-operate, don't respond
honestly and refuse to accept the implications of the exercise.

Practitioners are largely responsible for all this. Most experts like to protect their black arts, and much that's written on the subject concentrates heavily on issues of statistical analysis. Questionnaire design and question formulation, it is implied, are matters involving such arcane lore that they're unlikely to be properly understood, much less practised, by anyone lacking a PhD in experimental psychology.

Back to basics

Now statistical analysis *is* an important element of any survey, and one that we'll return to later on. Clearly, if the survey is to be based on a sample of employees, practitioners do need some knowledge of sample design and statistical significance. But the subtleties of statistical analysis are likely to be much less relevant in conducting an employee survey than in, say, market research or political opinion polls.

The formulation of questions and the overall design of the questionnaire, on the other hand, are likely to be critical. These are also much less straightforward than they might appear. We'll consider some of the potential problems that can arise through inappropriate or sloppy questionnaire design later. For the moment, it's sufficient to say that this is an area where, initially at least, you're probably best advised to employ an expert. Nevertheless, effective questionnaire design usually results more from experience, practice and trial-and-error than from the possession of any arcane knowledge. There are a few tricks and devices you can learn, and there are one or two basic pitfalls you can avoid. We'll discuss some of these later on in the book. Otherwise, though, it's a matter of finding out what works and what doesn't. And, since every questionnaire is likely to be different, even the expert may only discover all the problems as he or she goes along.

Getting involved

More important, even if you bring in an expert to design and run the survey – and there are other advantages in doing this, which we'll come to shortly – there's still no reason why you shouldn't get involved with the whole process. The expert may suggest that the procedure is so mysterious that you can contribute little or nothing, but it isn't. In practice, *you're* much more likely to understand the background to the survey, to be aware of potential pitfalls or areas of difficulty, and to know what issues are likely to be relevant to the workforce. No external expert, however well briefed, is likely to have such a thorough knowledge of internal practices and culture.

In my experience, internal managers frequently make a critical contribution; on occasion, their input can save the whole exercise from near-disaster. In some cases, this may be simply a matter of language. Words like 'department', 'function', 'unit', and 'sector' are often much more ambiguous than you'd think possible. Words like 'supervisor' and 'manager' can be even more so. All organizations have their own vocabularies and jargon, and if you get these wrong the survey results can be highly misleading. To take one simple example, the BBC calls its appraisal forms 'annual reports'. In that context, a question about how often employees read the annual report could easily be taken as a question about appraisal, whereas the surveyors might think they were asking how frequently employees look at the annual *BBC Handbook*. This kind of ambiguity might not even be spotted in piloting if respondents happily reply to the question they *think* is being asked.

In other cases, internal managers may well be able to make more extensive suggestions about material which should be added to (or indeed subtracted from) the questionnaire. If questions are being asked about motivation, for instance, it may well be obvious to any employee that these should mention particular unpleasant working practices or some element of the organization's remuneration system. It will not be obvious to external experts unless somebody is in a position to tell them.

The whole surveying process should therefore be carried out in close and direct consultation with appropriate internal managers. (We'll talk later on about just who these managers should be – this is often a bone of contention in its own right.) After all, it's the managers who are going to have to act on the results of the survey once they've gathered the data. Even if the external experts are able to assist and support the implementation process – still comparatively uncommon among consultants who perceive themselves merely as researchers – the internal management will still carry the responsibility. It's crucial, therefore, that managers find the survey useful, workable and appropriate, and that, above all, *it provides them with all the information they need to take action.* If the survey isn't going to fulfil their needs, managers must be able to rectify this at the start, rather than discovering it only when the results come in.

So what is an employee survey?

We've decided what an employee survey isn't. It isn't black magic, practised only by a few initiates with awesome academic qualifications. It isn't an obscure process which is carried out on the organization's behalf but without its involvement. So what is it?

In simple terms, an employee survey is any form of systematic investigation of employees' opinions, behaviour, feelings, attitudes or beliefs. It may be an investigation of some specific element of the working environment, such as communications or the reward system. Alternatively, it may be a more general study of employees' motivation, their feelings about the organization or their attitudes to their work.

The use of employee surveys is becoming increasingly popular. However, these kinds of techniques have actually been around, both in the United States and in Great Britain, for a good few decades. In this country, various forms of employee survey were used as far back as the 1930s, and in the US their history is even longer. In some organizations, as we indicated in Chapter 1, their use is almost commonplace. IBM, for instance, has made regular use of attitude surveys since the early 1960s, allowing results to be compared over this whole period.

In general, though not invariably, an employee survey will include a formal written component – in other words, a questionnaire form which is completed by respondents themselves. However, a survey does not have to be (and in most cases *should* not be) conducted purely in this written form. Survey material can also be gathered through face-to-face interviews – either fully structured or semi-structured – and through group discussions or workshops. The precise format will depend on the nature and purpose of the survey, and we'll discuss this in more detail later. However, in many cases, assuming that the aim is to support practical organizational change rather than merely to provide research data, it will be appropriate to use a combination of all these approaches.

'Soft' and 'hard' data

This last point may come as a surprise to some readers. We are accustomed to think of surveys as formal structured questionnaires, completed either by ourselves or by interviewers on our behalf. We are not so accustomed to think seriously about the process of gathering information through unstructured, informal processes. After all, that's just 'soft' information, isn't it? It isn't statistical. It can't be validated or measured. It can't be turned into graphs. It's a method we all use, of course, but that's just because we don't know any better.

In fact, this kind of unstructured, informal, 'soft' data is likely to be a critical element of most practical employee surveys. Of course, formal questionnaires also have an important role to play. There's a need to provide a foundation of reliable, measurable data which can be used as the basis for less formal or more speculative enquiries. But if you're interested in doing anything more than simply conducting research – in other words, if you are really interested in implementing practical, lasting organizational changes – this kind of information is unlikely to be sufficient.

The simple fact is that no written questionnaire is likely to be detailed or flexible enough to take account of the wealth of subjective perceptions, nuances, minor concerns and niggles that comprise most people's responses to their working environment. And, while it may be possible to disregard these subtleties for the purposes of 'pure' research, any manager knows that they're precisely the things that cause problems when it comes to implementation.

If there's any doubt about this, let's take a simple example. Suppose your organization were contemplating relocation, perhaps out of London into the Midlands. You employ a significant proportion of highly skilled technical staff, so, if the exercise is to be viable, you need to ensure that at least a sizeable majority of your employees come with you. If they don't, you won't be able to recruit the necessary skills from scratch, and the time and costs involved in training new staff to the required level would be unacceptable. To find out whether relocation will be possible, you conduct a written survey among all your staff.

The results are encouraging. Over 80% of the key groups of employees indicate that, yes, they'll be happy to come with you, provided that you meet all their out-of-pocket relocation expenses, along with an additional financial inducement to compensate for the inconvenience. Fine, you think. You do the calculations, work out that the organization can afford to proceed along these lines, and begin the relocation process. And that's when the problems start. First, you get a small but significant minority of key staff complaining that, while you're meeting their relocation expenses, you're doing nothing about the problems of their children's education. Several have children within a year of crucial examinations. While they're happy to relocate, they don't want to do it yet. If they do, they want you to pay for additional coaching for the children to compensate. Or they want you to pay for them to relocate to rented accommodation while their families stay behind.

And then another group comes along. This one has aged or invalid relatives they need to look after. Yes, of course, they're happy to relocate, but you'll have to do something about the relatives. Perhaps pay for them to come too. Or finance some additional care. Or . . . And at that point another group appears. Yes, this group's happy to relocate too, but they've got to consider their spouses' careers. If they were to relocate to some mid-point, say in the northern Home Counties, would the organization be willing to reimburse the additional travel expenses incurred? Alternatively, is the organization able to offer the spouse a job? Or . . .

By this time, the relocation has begun to look much less straightforward. All the original calculations have gone out of the window. If the organization refuses to agree to these requests, then it may fail to take a sufficient number of key employees with it. Even if it just turns down a few of them, the resulting poor internal publicity and drop in morale might be enough to persuade others that they don't want to move. Beleaguered on all sides, you curse the day you ever thought of conducting a survey.

Of course, a better prepared survey might well have covered some of the above issues and enabled managers to predict some of these minority responses. But it's a safe bet that, in any major change exercise, there'll be a significant number of factors which the survey has failed to cover. Some of these factors may be trivial, some may apply only to one or two individuals. Nevertheless, particularly in the pressure-cooker atmosphere of change, they can assume a disproportionate significance which may undermine all your careful plans.

The truth is that no written survey, however well planned and constructed, is ever going to cover all the possible permutations and subtleties of human response. And even if it were possible to construct a survey in this way, the resulting document would probably be so long and unwieldy that no-one would want to complete it anyway. If you're intending to use the survey as the basis for making practical, workable management decisions, it is always better to supplement the written survey with a sequence of more informal, open-ended discussions which can allow employees to explore *all* their possible responses. You'll often find that, when individuals come to talk about issues in this way, they uncover thoughts, attitudes and beliefs which even *they* didn't know they had. In group discussions, particularly, one person's responses may often spark off thought in others: 'Oh, my goodness, that's true – I'd never thought what we'd do with Great Uncle Albert . . . ' or 'Blimey, I'd forgotten that – Kylie'll be in her GCSE year as well by then . . . '

We'll discuss this whole process of information gathering in more detail shortly. For the moment, let's just point out that gathering information to inform management decisions is a very different process from gathering data purely for research purposes. In one sense, it may be a less rigorous process. But it usually needs to be a much more flexible, responsive process, able to deal with people as individuals rather than simply as statistics.

The benefits of a written questionnaire

This is not intended to imply that formal written surveys have no place in gathering information from employees. On the contrary, while it's certainly possible to gather information solely through verbal discussions (and one of the earliest UK surveys, conducted by Winifred Raphael of the National Institute of Industrial

Psychology in the 1930s, did just that), formal, written questionnaires are likely to form the backbone of most employee surveys.

Although comparatively inflexible, the written questionnaire
does have a number of crucial benefits. First, it can be very
precisely designed to extract particular kinds of data. While an
open-ended interview may be very useful for uncovering unexpected or tangential – but still critical – information, it is often much
less good at providing precise answers to precise questions. A
skilled interviewer may be able to pin down respondents, but it's
all too easy for answers to be vague, evasive or downright irrel-
evant. This is particularly true when the interview is covering
'difficult' areas – for example, personal or emotional responses to
a situation, or critical responses to individuals. In the context of
an interview, people are often reluctant to say, 'Actually, I feel
really miserable in this organization' or 'Well, it would be all right
if I didn't have to work for that miserable toad . . . ' Often,
they're even reluctant to say things like 'Well, I think working
practices in this organization are really inefficient' or 'No, actually,
since you ask, I *don't* like the overtime system in this company.'

In general – though we can all think of exceptions – we like to
be liked, and we're very nervous about speaking ill of other people
and their efforts. We usually feel uncomfortable even about saying
anything that might be *interpreted* as a criticism, let alone coming
straight out and saying what we think. Even people who are
constantly complaining or carping often prefer to do it in an
abstract way – 'The trouble with this place . . . ' or 'One day, I'll
tell that so-and-so exactly what I think of him . . . ' – rather than
making open direct criticism of individuals. This is the reason why
interpreting written appraisals or references is so often a matter
of discriminating between various levels of blandness. And it's
the reason why people tend to respond evasively in face-to-face
interviews or group discussions, however skilfully these are run.

By contrast, written questionnaires are usually anonymous and
so encourage honest responses. Even if they aren't anonymous –
and occasionally this isn't possible or desirable – people often feel
more comfortable expressing their feelings in writing. Furthermore, most survey questionnaires are based primarily around a
sequence of multiple-choice questions.

We've already touched on the main disadvantage of these –
they tend to be inflexible. They exclude complex or subtle

responses. As we all know from filling in such questionnaires – from sophisticated personality inventories to 'Are you a great lover?' magazine quizzes – we often want to reply, 'Well, it depends what you mean by . . . ' or 'I'd like to answer something *between* iii) and iv) actually'.

On the other hand, this inflexibility is also the strength of multiple-choice questions. The respondent is forced to come off the fence and express an opinion. Of course, he or she may still lie (although many people are reluctant to lie too blatantly in writing!), but it is not possible to evade the issue or just provide an anodyne or ambivalent answer. We'll look at the detailed issues of wording and phrasing in a later chapter.

Of course, this doesn't mean that questionnaires should be composed exclusively of multiple-choice questions. Most include a mixture of these and more open-ended questions. However, although open questions may provide valuable supplementary information, it is usually the multiple-choice questions which provide the data which could not be collected so effectively in other ways.

Combining survey methods

Different methods of collecting data – written questionnaires, interviews, group discussions, etc. – provide different kinds of information. If you want to gain a detailed, three-dimensional picture of what's going on, then you probably need to use a variety of approaches. One may give you clear, comparatively unequivocal views. Another will enable you to sketch in the important nuances and details. Taken together, they should provide sufficient reliable information for you to make precise and appropriate management decisions.

Summary

- Effective data collection always requires a high level of forethought, experience and skill

- Unlike interviewing, designing questionnaires is not a skill which personnel departments are normally expected to possess
- Employee surveys seldom involve the higher reaches of statistical analysis – don't let yourself be blinded with science
- Even if you use a consultant, keep involved throughout
- Keep managers informed – it is they who will have to act on the survey results
- Most employee surveys include interviews and multiple-choice questionnaires – you need to obtain both 'hard' and 'soft' data
- Always remember that surveys are intended not solely to obtain information but to help managers make decisions.

Chapter Three

Where Do I Start?

"'Begin at the beginning," the King said, gravely, "and go on till you come to the end: then stop."'

Lewis Carroll, Alice in Wonderland

The King's advice to Alice is all very well. However, the manager who's decided to carry out an employee survey has first of all to decide where the beginning actually is. How should the idea be introduced to the workforce? Is it necessary to consult the trade unions or other representative bodies? What management groups need to be involved? Is the survey likely to tread on the toes of other management functions? Does the process have sufficient support and commitment from senior management? And, above all, is there sufficient will and energy from all parties to ensure that the organization responds promptly and appropriately to the results of the survey?

This whole process is a minefield, and the manager initially has only the vaguest notion of where to tread. And yet, as we discussed in Chapter 1, it's difficult to set out across this threatening terrain unless you've got at least a broad idea of where you're trying to get to. Let's take some time to consider how you begin to develop an itinerary.

Starting out

You're at the point where you've decided that a survey would be appropriate. Most likely, this is because you've been keeping an eye on the indices we discussed in Chapter 1 and you now begin

41

to feel that you've got some kind of potential problem. Or your decision may be more proactive. Perhaps you want to introduce some new management system – pay, appraisal, career development – and you want to test the water before you make the necessary investment. Perhaps you've already introduced some changes, and you want to see how they've been received. Perhaps you simply want to gain a better understanding of how the workforce feels about some particular issues, in order to inform your future management decision-making.

The next major question you need to consider is whether the cost and effort of a survey can really be justified. This is a critical – and often underestimated – issue, which we'll be coming back to in subsequent chapters as we look in more detail at the survey process. All too often, managers take the view that a survey is bound to be a good thing and that, really, it can't be all that much trouble, can it? It's just getting a few people to fill in a few forms, a bit of analysis and there you are. Can't cost all that much. Bit of management time, printing the forms, getting the computer people to analyse it – say a few hundred pounds.

Costs and benefits

In reality, unless you've been through the process before, you'll almost certainly underestimate the time, effort, costs and problems involved. The whole process is likely to be much longer and more complex than you imagine. Even if you don't run into unexpected and major problems – and you'll be lucky to avoid all of them – everything will take two or three times longer than seems possible, you'll need to involve far more people than you ever expect, and you'll encounter all kinds of minor disputes and quibbles about the survey design, the wording of questions, the structure of the survey sample and a hundred other issues that you'd never even thought about.

Let's just take an example, based on my own experience. You might decide that, once you've got agreement in principle from the rest of the management team, then you can take full charge of the survey design, probably with expert help. At the end of the design stage and once all the relevant parties have been consulted, you'll go back to the management team with the draft questionnaire as agreed between yourself and the experts. The management team will then give their final assent that the survey can proceed. However, that should be just a formality: the individual views of the management team have already been incorporated into the design.

Except, of course, it doesn't work out like that. You may have already consulted the members of the management team individually. Collectively they may express different views. The Finance Director may suddenly pipe up with, 'You know, I've been thinking about this, and I'm not sure that Question 6 really covers *all* the salary issues we're interested in . . . ' The Sales Director then sees an opportunity to raise something that he's vaguely thought about, but hadn't felt able to raise at such a late stage. 'Well, now you come to mention it, I must admit I'm not sure that Question 15 really asks what we want about the company's image.' And before you know it, the whole team is pulling apart the questionnaire, some to score points, others to protect their backs or territory, others because they genuinely want to improve the survey, even if they've left it rather late in the day to do so.

At the end of the meeting you're back at square one. The management team have refused to give their assent 'just until these one or two little niggles are ironed out'. The whole survey is delayed. You've got to go back to the designers to re-think the questionnaire, perhaps trying to reconcile three or four contradictory views. Not only that, you'll also have to go back to all those people whom you originally consulted to get *their* views on the proposed changes. Suddenly, the survey has been set back six weeks and the costs have doubled. And, in the light of that, your original decision about the justification of conducting the survey begins to look rather more shaky . . .

This may be an extreme example, but it's one based on experience. Snares and pitfalls may be waiting at any stage of the process, however simple or trivial they appear at the start. Even if these problems don't raise their heads, there'll be other delays. If you decide to consult with the trade unions or line managers about the questionnaire design, you can bet that they'll take three times longer than expected to get the draft back to you – 'Sorry it took so long, but we couldn't give you a view until Ronnie was back from holiday, and then Brian was off on that training course for three days, and by the time we'd got our notes typed up . . . '

The safest rule of thumb when estimating the costs of a survey is to make a careful inventory of each stage – including all the apparently trivial or straightforward ones – that you're likely to have to go through in setting up and running the survey. When you've done that, then add another, say, 30% to account for all the potential delays and problems that might arise. Use *that* figure to decide whether the survey can be justified or not. If you're very lucky, you might find that you come in well under budget. If you're very unfortunate, you might find that it takes still longer and costs more even than this inflated figure. But at least you shouldn't have underestimated *too* wildly.

Longer-term implications

You should also remember that the ultimate costs won't be confined to the survey itself. We've already mentioned the risks of failing to act on the results. So, when you're considering how much the survey is likely to cost, you shouldn't forget to include the costs of longer-term changes that occur in response to it. If you don't think about these resulting costs at the start, the consequences can be disastrous. There are numerous instances where the Chief Executive has ended up saying, 'Yes, I know I said you could conduct the survey, Bill. And I know the results indicate that 95% of the workforce is unhappy with the new bonus scheme. But we simply can't *afford* to make these kinds of changes now we've invested so much . . . '

Of course, this is probably the most difficult area to predict. After all, if you knew what the results of the survey were going to be beforehand, you wouldn't need to carry it out. To some extent, you have to work in the dark – it's always possible that the survey might indicate the need for some unexpectedly major change. But you can usually make some broad estimate of the likely costs of the survey results, and identify the costs of the 'worst case'. For example, if you're conducting a survey about attitudes to a newly introduced remuneration scheme, the worst outcome would probably be if the survey identified a need to scrap and replace the system entirely. In practice, you'll probably have to do little more than tinker with minor aspects of the system, but at least you're prepared for the worst.

In other words, when you're calculating the potential costs of the survey, you need to ensure that you've taken account of *all* the implications. You'll probably end up with a range of possible long-term costs. At one extreme, if you're lucky, you may need to take no action whatsoever. Your survey may simply confirm that all is right with the world and no changes are needed. In that case, the only costs are those involved in actually conducting the survey. In the worst case, you might find that you need to make major changes in virtually every aspect of the areas covered. Make a reasonable estimate of the horrendous costs involved – you can always console yourself that the long-term costs of *not* making the changes would have been even worse. You can also make some predictions about the most likely results of the survey – you may, for example, already have a reasonable idea about where change is needed.

With this range of figures, you can then make an honest and full appraisal of whether or not the survey can be justified. You may certainly be willing to accept the probable costs of the survey, but are you also willing to accept the 'worse-case' costs, if that's the way the results come out? If you feel that you wouldn't be able to afford to respond to an expressed desire for major change, it might well be better not to raise the issue in the first place. Perhaps you should restrict the survey to those areas where you could afford to make changes, if necessary.

These questions are complex, and there are no simple answers. Much will depend on the particular circumstances. But the simple rule is that, when conducting employee surveys, you should always be prepared to put your money where your mouth is. If you know beforehand that the organization couldn't afford to restructure the entire remuneration system, then don't offer that as an option in the questionnaire. If you know that major capital investment is out of the question, then don't encourage responses that demand such investment. It is all too easy, in designing a questionnaire, to feel that you have to incorporate every option, so as to get as accurate a picture as possible of respondents' views. In practice, questionnaire design, like politics, is the art of the possible. If you encourage demands which cannot be fulfilled, whether for financial or other reasons, this can only bring you problems later on.

Benefits

Against all these various probable and possible costs, you'll then have to weigh up the likely benefits of the questionnaire. Again, this is by no means an easy task: if you could predict the results of the survey beforehand, there'd be no point in conducting it. At one extreme, it's possible that the survey might identify a potential major problem and the means of resolving it. It might be possible to trace declining productivity to widespread dissatisfaction with a particular production process. You change the process, and productivity increases.

In practice, of course, things are rarely so straightforward, although I can think of one or two cases where surveys have led to precisely this kind of dramatic saving. Even if the results *are* as neat as this, you couldn't have predicted it beforehand with any certainty. In most cases, the benefits accruing from surveys are much less quantifiable. The results will probably indicate some areas where changes can usefully be made, and this will enable you to make some improvements which do lead to, say, increased commitment. But the increase will probably not be dramatic, and may well be attributable to other factors. In the end, while you may be sure that the survey has contributed to the improvements, you may be very hard pressed to actually put a figure on the financial benefits that have accrued.

At the opposite extreme, it's also possible that the survey might indicate that everything is hunky-dory and that no real change is necessary. In one sense, this is a pleasing result – everyone likes to have confirmation that they're actually doing everything alright after all. On the other hand, this is often the result that causes most embarrassment to the manager who's been responsible for commissioning the survey in the first place. The manager can hear (either actual or imagined) colleagues muttering, 'All that money, just to tell us we were doing everything right all the time. *I* could've told them that, if they'd only bothered to ask . . . ' Of course, this is usually nonsense. Very few managers are totally confident that they're doing everything right (and those that are most confident often have least cause to be). And if you *can* be confident that your current approach is successful, this will probably help management make future decisions with more boldness.

The benefits of such confirmation may be very real, even they're unquantifiable.

The key questions

In short, it's notoriously difficult to quantify the likely benefits of an employee survey in advance (and it's sometimes hard even to quantify them afterwards). However, in deciding whether or not to conduct a survey, there are two basic questions you should ask yourself:

- Is the survey likely to tell me something I don't know, with reasonable certainty, already?
- If so, is this information going to assist the organization in making more effective management decisions?

If the answer to both these questions is yes, then the survey will almost certainly bring financial benefits, however unquantifiable. Clearly, you will have to decide whether these benefits are likely, on balance, to outweigh the costs of the survey. This will often not be an easy judgement; one of the reasons for spelling out these problems in detail is to offer food for thought to those managers who lightly assume that a survey must automatically be a 'good thing'.

Who owns the survey?

There are still one or two more issues that you need to consider before you leap into the fray – issues which are often forgotten. In my experience they're often the factors that fatally undermine the value of a survey.

The first of these is *commitment*. If the survey is to be truly effective, all those involved need to be fully committed to its aims and operation. This may seem obvious, and that may be why it's frequently taken for granted. But in fact you can't simply assume that everyone will share your views about the benefits and value of the survey.

If the Chief Executive wants to commission or conduct a survey, of course, then he or she can usually manage to insist on support from others. Even then, those actually responsible for implementing the decision can often undermine it if they lack commitment or simply don't understand the aim of the exercise. In the anecdotal example at the beginning of Chapter 1, the Chief Executive had come up with the idea, but hadn't bothered to explain his motives or objectives (probably because he didn't know himself). As a result, the Personnel Manager who ultimately got landed with the problem was sent on a fool's errand. In other cases I've come across, the manager responsible for implementing the idea has either misunderstood the senior manager's reasons for proposing a survey or, worse still, has deliberately sabotaged the exercise, perceiving it as a waste of time and money.

If a more junior manager wants to conduct or commission a survey, then he or she will have even greater problems. By their nature, employee surveys tend to impact across numerous departments and functions, and it's difficult for any single manager to retain full ownership. The survey might, for example, be initiated by the personnel function, but it is likely to cover issues relating to a variety of line functions. If it deals with areas such as pay, it may also carry implications for the finance function. And the simple fact of conducting a survey, whatever its subject matter, may involve administrative functions, information technology and the communications or public-relations function.

All of these functions may want to be involved, and all will have their own particular axes to grind. If you're not careful, the original objectives of the survey may well be forgotten under a flood of 'We must include a question about . . . .' or 'We can't ask about that without also asking . . . ' You might even find that other managers feel that *they* should be running the survey. The communications people may claim that this is their field, and what are personnel doing sticking their noses in, anyway? The line managers may claim that, since they're the ones who have to live with the results, they should be in charge. All of these arguments have merit. The trouble is that no single survey can bear the weight of so many good intentions.

And this may not be the only problem. You must also recognize that employee surveys tend to be threatening. For example, if managers feel insecure about their position or performance, the last thing they want is to consult the views of their employees.

There is always a fear, stated or unstated, that the survey will expose the manager's failings. In some cases, of course, particularly in surveys of management style or practices, this can actually happen. If significant dissatisfaction is expressed by the members of a particular department, senior managers may well begin to ask questions about how the department is managed.

However, these are extreme cases – and probably cases where senior management had suspicions anyway. More commonly, the survey is concerned with general issues, which reflect on overall company policies or practices, rather than on the performance of an individual manager. Nonetheless, this won't prevent the insecure from worrying, and worry can easily turn into opposition.

A colleague of mine recently worked at an organization which had expressed interest in conducting a survey about internal customer service. The initial contacts with the organization had sounded promising, and the manager involved – who happened to be the Communications Director – had been very enthusiastic about what might be achieved.

My colleague had listened intently, and then asked, 'And what other departments do you think should be involved?'

'Other departments?' asked the Communications Director. 'What do you mean? It's nothing to do with them, is it? It's a communications issue.'

'Well, perhaps,' agreed my colleague, deciding to put this issue aside for the moment. 'Anyway,' he said, to change the subject, 'when would you want the survey to be carried out?'

'Ah well, that depends,' said the Communications Director. 'You see, I don't myself have formal authorization to spend that kind of money. I'll need to take it to the management team to get their agreement. But that's just a formality. After all, it's obvious that we need to do it, and they'll defer to my judgement as the expert in the area, so long as I can demonstrate the benefits. So, once we've got their agreement, then we can go ahead almost immediately . . . '

Needless to say, the survey did not go ahead 'almost immediately'; it still hasn't gone ahead to this day. When the idea was mooted at the management meeting, the Communications Director found himself facing all the problems mentioned above. Some managers felt threatened by the survey – it was bound to expose their failings in the customer-service area, wasn't it? Others felt that the Communications Director was overstepping his remit: surely employee surveys were a personnel responsibility? Why hadn't line managers been told about this? The Managing Director simply thought the whole thing was a waste of time and money, and refused to be convinced by the Communications Director's mass of elegant diagrams. As a result, the project was indefinitely shelved. My colleague's pessimism had proved well founded.

In this case, the management team were pretty much unanimous in their opposition to the survey, though their individual motives were quite varied. As such, they had no problem in blocking it. But even if there is broad agreement to the idea of a survey, it is still possible for one anxious or disgruntled manager to undermine the exercise. Surveys can be sabotaged in a hundred and one ways. If the survey initiator or designer is not fully *au fait* with the issues in different departments, the malcontent manager might encourage the inclusion of supplementary questions about highly contentious but comparatively unimportant issues: 'I know the survey's primarily about pay, but I think we ought to ask something about office accommodation, just for completeness . . . ' As a result, the respondents get caught up in expressing their feelings about the subsidiary issue and ignore the primary one.

More straightforwardly, an anxious manager might simply spread a few inaccurate rumours among the workforce about the motives for the survey: 'Well, I suppose I shouldn't really say this, but the MD gave me the impression that redundancies might be on the cards, and if that's the case I suppose it'll be difficult for management to ignore the views you express about the company in the survey. Still, don't let that worry you. It's important that you say what you think . . . ' – with the result that, of course, no one's prepared to express an honest opinion in case it's used in evidence against them.

Getting commitment

First, and probably most important, all relevant managers must be fully involved in the exercise right from the start. From the moment that you decide that it would be worthwhile conducting an employee survey, you should begin to consult with senior management and line managers in all the areas that are likely to be covered.

The extent of the consultation will depend on the culture of the organization and the nature of the proposed survey. However, at the very least, you should set out what you would like to do, explain the likely costs and benefits and indicate as clearly as you can the likely (and conceivable) impact on the manager in question. And, as a general rule, don't be dishonest. If you feel that the survey is likely to pose any kind of the threat to the manager – if, for instance, it may encourage comment on the manager's role or performance – then, for Heaven's sake, say so and explain why you think this is necessary (as tactfully as you can, needless to say). If you don't, the chances are that the manager will work it out anyway soon enough, and then the benefits of consultation will be lost.

Second, as part of this consultation process, encourage input from the other managers. This has to be handled quite carefully. The danger is that you'll either lose ownership of the project or end up trying to reconcile a dozen contradictory ideas or approaches. Without wishing to go too far into the intricacies of organizational politics, I've generally found that the most successful approach is first of all to obtain the support and commitment of top management – either the Chief Executive or whichever senior manager is appropriate in the circumstances. Once that support is obtained, it confirms your own position as champion of the exercise and you'll have a much easier time maintaining control.

And there's no doubt that a single, identifiable champion is likely to be critical to the effectiveness of this kind of exercise. Certainly, you should involve as many managers as are necessary. Certainly, if it's appropriate in your organization, you should set up a working party or steering group representing these managers, who can keep a watching brief on how the survey develops. This is often a helpful device for allaying some of those anxieties and fears that we talked about earlier. But there should always be one figure who drives the whole process and who ensures that it meets its specified deadlines and objectives. Otherwise, the exercise will fragment, with different managers firmly grinding their own particular axes. If this happens, even if the survey manages to get off the ground, it's unlikely to produce results which genuinely improve the organization's decision-making capability.

Commitment from trade unions

Before we move on to the survey proper, there's one other area of consultation which we should touch upon. Just as surveys can easily be sabotaged by managers, they can equally be sabotaged by the workforce and its representatives. The representatives may be trade unions, staff associations or internal staff consultative bodies. If they are unhappy with what you are setting out to do, they can cast a decidedly malign influence.

In theory, you might think that such bodies should welcome employee surveys. After all, their role is to represent the views of the workforce – surely they should encourage an exercise which is designed to facilitate the expression of those views? In practice, this is also usually the case. Most trade unions, for example, now recognize the value of surveys and, all else being equal, prefer to work alongside management to ensure that the exercise is as useful as possible. But managers should recognize that employee surveys, like any other form of management-inspired consultation, have the potential to undermine the role of unions and other similar bodies.

Indeed, it's not unknown for employee surveys to be used deliberately to undermine the effectiveness of representative bodies – by going over their heads directly to the workforce. Where management suspects, for example, that the union is not accurately representing the workforce's views or strength of opinion, surveys can test this hypothesis. If the results contradict the union's assertions, its position becomes untenable, unless the integrity of the survey can be challenged.

Yet even if management is commissioning a survey for less Machiavellian motives, many unions will still see it as a potential usurper of their role as the primary medium for management-employee communication. In many organizations, this exclusive role has been pretty much undermined already by the use of other communications media – newsletters, consultative committees, videos, briefing groups, quality circles and so on. Nonetheless, no union worth its salt is going to allow a further erosion of its role (however hypothetical) without at least attempting to make some industrial-relations capital from the process. It's for this reason that many unions will raise initial objections about the concept of surveying – that it's unethical, intrusive, misleading or whatever.

Most of these accusations should have little substance, so long as the survey is conducted professionally. No survey should intrude into employees' private affairs (unless the employees choose to volunteer the information) and no one should be compelled to take part against his or her will. In this context, and provided that it is competently designed and administered, the survey should be above reproach.

But that's not really the point. The union is likely to have its own agenda – it needs to demonstrate to its members that it has a role to play, that it's actively representing their interests and that it isn't letting management take advantage of it or its members. So, just as you'll need to take account of managers' concerns and anxieties, you'll need to take account of the union's needs.

As with the managers, the simplest and most effective approach is likely to be early involvement of the union or equivalent in the survey process. In other words, once you've got senior management support for the idea, and as soon as you start to involve the other managers, you should also start to involve the unions or other representative bodies. Tell them clearly what you're up to. Explain the potential benefits to the organization and to their members, but also indicate as honestly as you're able if there are any areas of potential concern. Again, if you don't reveal these at the start, you can bet that they'll emerge soon enough anyway. And, most important of all, encourage the union to have an input. If there's a working party or steering group, invite the union to take part. After all, you should have nothing to hide. The process will all be public anyway. So don't engage in unnecessary secrecy or exclusivity.

In the end, it'll be to your benefit. The union may well be much closer to the grassroots than you are – they may well have their own ideas about the issues and about what the survey should cover. And, if they know their stuff, this could save you invaluable time at the design stage. Furthermore, with the union actively involved from the start, it'll be much harder for them to reject the results or question the integrity of the survey, if they happen to be unhappy with the way things turn out. In the end, as with the managers, commitment is all-important. The earlier you can obtain commitment to the survey process, the easier it will be to ensure that it leads to real, practical results which are accepted by everyone.

Summary

- Successful surveys depend on good preparation beforehand
- Draw up a careful assessment of likely costs and benefits before you start
- Make sure the survey is going to tell you something useful that you don't know (or strongly suspect) already
- Encourage input from others, but let one person keep driving the exercise forward
- Get the commitment of colleagues, senior management and the unions
- Commitment must extend beyond the survey itself to implementing the necessary action.

Chapter Four

Designing the Survey – The First Steps

'O! that a man might know
The end of this day's business, ere it come;
But sufficeth that the day will end,
And then the end is known'

Julius Caesar V. i. 123ff.

Brutus' lament has been echoed by many managers setting out to design and conduct an employee survey. We're once again face to face with the old research paradox – that you don't know what you're looking for until you've found it. And because you don't know what you're looking for, you don't even know how to begin the hunt. Faced with this dilemma, many managers just plunge straight in, and then they're disappointed because the survey results don't give them the kinds of information they need. How do you avoid this outcome?

Preparing for the survey

For clarity, let's take a specific example. Suppose you've noticed that both turnover and absenteeism have been noticeably higher in the Grommet Finishing Department than elsewhere in the organization over the past year. There's no obvious reason why this should be the case. You subscribe to the Grommet Finishers' Salary Club, and you believe that your salaries are pretty much competitive. You don't seem to have too much difficulty in recruiting skilled grommet finishers. You conduct exit interviews, but they have proved singularly unrevealing. You've talked to the

55

local managers and supervisors, but they've only offered fairly bland responses. They've made one or two comments about unsatisfactory production processes, but you suspect they're just grinding familiar axes about the need for more capital investment.

Finally, you've also looked back at the records for previous years, and you've noticed what seems to be a trend. Four years ago, absenteeism and turnover among grommet finishers were no higher than elsewhere. Since then, absenteeism and turnover have risen gradually, year on year, until there is a large disparity between this department and the rest. On this basis, therefore, you believe that a survey might be able to give you an insight into the real causes of the problem.

So where do you go from here? We'll assume that you've taken the advice of the previous chapter and have evaluated the likely costs and benefits of a survey. This kind of evaluation should be an iterative process. In other words, you should keep reassessing the situation as your plans for the survey become more detailed. You might, for example, ultimately decide that you will be unable to obtain any useful information except by conducting a much more extensive or complex (and therefore costly) survey than you originally envisaged. If this is the case, then you might well decide to abandon the idea, even at a comparatively late stage.

Focussing the survey

If you decide to go ahead, the first question you need to ask is: what issues is the survey going to cover? The answer may seem obvious. After all, you know what the problem appears to be. You know which department the problem's in. You might even have some suspicions about what the causes are. Yet this question is rarely as straightforward as it appears. First of all, the causes of even an apparently straightforward problem might actually be complex and multifarious. I've come across examples where high turnover or absenteeism has been caused by a combination of factors ranging from dislike of an autocratic supervisor through unhappiness with production methods to irritation with the office accommodation. Of course, some of these factors may be linked. It's quite possible that, say, employees would be much happier about production methods if it wasn't for the autocratic supervisor. Or that the dissatisfaction with the office accommodation is merely a symptom of wider discontents with the supervisor or production methods.

This interdependency makes it harder to disentangle the real roots of the problem. It's quite likely that *all* the factors contribute, to a greater or lesser degree, to the overall problem. If you assume there's only one cause, you may well succeed only in alleviating, rather than solving, the problem.

We'll look in a moment at how you might begin to investigate some of the deeper issues. For now, though, the primary message is: don't take anything for granted. Don't assume that the apparent issue or the apparent cause of problems is the only or even the primary one. Be prepared for the possibility that there may be several factors involved, perhaps interconnected and of varying significance, but all contributing.

Incidentally, although we've been concentrating in this section on a situation where management commissions a survey in response to a perceived problem, the same rule holds good when management has proactively commissioned a survey for its own purposes. Again, don't take anything for granted. If you're conducting a survey about, say, relocation or pay, you may think you know what the issues are; your employees may well have different ideas. If the nature and the content of the survey are overly constrained by your own preconceptions, you might as well not bother. It's much cheaper simply to act on your prejudices at the start!

The survey process

This is all very well, you may say, but it just brings us back to our central paradox. You can't conduct the survey effectively unless you know what the issues are, and you don't know what the issues are until you've conducted the survey. So where do you break into this vicious circle?

In practice, it doesn't much matter where, as long as you keep an open mind and make sure that the research process is iterative. In other words, you start off with one or more working hypotheses which you then proceed to test out and develop. The trick is to do as much of this as you possibly can before you get into the formal survey. By the time you reach the written (and therefore comparatively expensive) stage, you'll have a much better idea about the accuracy of your hypotheses and you'll probably have expanded them to include one or two other issues you hadn't thought of at the start.

To achieve this, employee surveys should normally be conducted in three broad stages, as follows:

Stage 1 – Preparation
Aim: to test and explore preliminary hypotheses, assumptions or issues
Style: informal, open, participative
Methods: probably a combination of interviews and/or group discussions.

Stage 2 – Formal Survey
Aim: formally to test and explore main hypotheses, assumptions or issues, with the usual aim of producing quantitative findings
Style: usually formal, closed, comparatively non-participative
Methods: probably some form of written self-completed questionnaire or possibly highly structured interviews.

Stage 3 – Follow Up
Aim: to explore details or aspects of the findings arising from Stage 2
Style: informal, open, participative
Methods: interviews or group discussion.

We might call this the *hourglass* approach, with the two 'open' ends sandwiching the 'closed' formal gathering of statistical data. We'll come to Stages 2 and 3 shortly. For the moment, though, let's look at Stage 1, the preparation stage, in more detail. And, for clarity, let's go back to the problem with our grommet finishers.

Developing preliminary theories

The causes of our problems are not immediately obvious. Nevertheless, we start off with some basic assumptions. The first is that the trend isn't just coincidence, that there is actually *some* reason (or reasons) for it. If we wished, we could conduct a test of statistical significance, to check the likelihood that this really is a significant trend rather than a coincidental blip. In practice, most managers won't bother. Given the potential costs of conducting surveys, even the most enthusiastic manager is unlikely to act – or get support from the organization – until the trend is pretty much evident to the naked eye.

We also assume, before we embark on our survey, that there is some *particular* cause for the trend within the organization, rather than a more general issue relating to the nature of the job or the profession. Beyond these two basic assumptions, you might have a number of more specific theories which you would also want to explore in more detail. For example, you may be aware that the Head Grommet Finisher is a rather abrasive character. Although he's widely respected for his grommet-finishing skills, he's also widely feared and, you suspect, often disliked. Although you've received no particular complaints about him, you believe that he may be a contributory factor.

You're also aware that, although working conditions in the organization are generally fairly good, the Grommet Finishing Room is less satisfactory than most. It's the oldest part of the site and is fairly run down. It has no air conditioning and can get very hot in summer. Again, you suspect that this is a contributory factor.

Finally, you know that the grommet finishers have been under a rather high level of pressure compared with other parts of the operation. Over the past few years, the organization has gradually been increasing automation across the production process. The result is that many parts of the plant are now highly automated, with attendant increases in productivity. However, because of a combination of technical difficulties and shortage of capital investment, it's not yet proved possible to automate the grommet finishing process. The grommet finishers have therefore been under considerable pressure to match productivity levels in other parts of the operation. This also could be a contributory factor.

In summary, as a result of your initial musings, perhaps reinforced by a few informal words with the relevant line managers, you've come up with a number of broad theories. As a basis for further investigation, therefore, you take the view that:

- the turnover and absenteeism trends are significant
- these trends relate to causes specific to the organization, rather than to general conditions of the trade
- the trends could be related to a number of factors, including: local management/supervisory style
working conditions
changing working practices.

At this stage, you're not sure if all (or any) of these theories are true. If they *are* true, you have little idea of their relative importance. You don't, for example, know whether all your suggested causes are contributing equally to the problem, or whether one particular cause is more important. And, above all, you don't know whether this list is comprehensive. In other words, there may be factors or causes which you haven't yet considered and which may be more important than those above. If there are further significant factors which you fail to address in your survey, your findings may be of little use in resolving the problem. The first stage is to test and investigate your hypotheses in more detail, using the open, participative methods – Stage 1 of the hourglass process.

The exploratory stage

In general, this initial testing will be carried out using a small number of semi-structured interviews. You don't really want to conduct two written surveys if you can avoid it – not least because they're costly and time-consuming. Since you're mixing with the employees fairly closely anyway, there are more effective ways of getting an informal feel for what's going on. Finally, there's always a risk that a written survey is going to spread suspicion and concern amongst those surveyed. You don't really want to risk this until you're fairly certain you're on the right lines. An ill-chosen question at this early stage could provoke a level of suspicion or resentment that would undermine the findings of the more carefully considered formal survey.

Before we consider how our interviews should be set up and conducted, let's just pause to give some thought to who should conduct them. Is this the point, you may ask, where you should make a tactical withdrawal from the affair and bring in a third-party expert?

Using consultants

In practice, there's no straightforward answer to this question. It will depend on your own feelings, on the organization's business and culture, on the nature of the issue or problem under investigation, and – not to put too fine a point on it – on the finances available. If this is the first time that the organization has considered such a survey, then your colleagues and bosses may well have offered only fairly equivocal commitment at this stage. It may therefore be difficult to justify the costs of bringing in a consultant until you've a better idea of the issues and the benefits that might result. Similarly, you might feel that it's best to treat the matter informally, so as not to arouse unnecessary concern from the workforce. In this context, the arrival of a smartly suited consultant could easily send out the wrong signals.

On the other hand, there can be definite benefits in using an expert third-party even at this stage. Since good consultants act independently – and are *perceived* as being independent – they can play the role of 'honest broker' between management and unions. Since they can also assure confidentiality, employees will often answer questions far more frankly than if they are dealing directly with management.

Although managers are paying for consultants, therefore, they should resist the temptation to try and get them to divulge sources of important information. The only result of this will be to ruin the atmosphere of trust they have built up in their interview sessions. By respecting confidentiality, on the other hand, consultants will get far more honest replies to their questions – which is considerably more useful to employers in the long run.

Furthermore, of course, consultants can bring their expertise to the design and conducting of open-ended semi-structured interviews. Such expertise is often underrated. Managers, especially personnel managers, often think: 'Interviews? Do them all the time. This'll be no problem.' They realize only afterwards that either they've gathered very little real data or that the material they have collected is too confused and ill-structured to be useful. By contrast, a skilled research interviewer is usually able to obtain a significant mass of valuable information even from comparatively few interview sessions.

We will return to the issue of consultants in the next chapter, where the even more specialized skill of designing a written questionnaire is discussed.

Putting your cards on the table?

Whoever carries out the exercise, however, the process will be broadly the same. This is the open-ended, participative end of the hourglass. You will carry out a number of fairly informal, open discussions with selected respondents, either one-to-one or in groups. In practice, it is usually most helpful, first of all, to conduct two or three interviews with the supervisors and relevant line managers. In our hypothetical example, you might talk to the Grommet Finishing Manager and the two departmental supervisors. The aim of these initial interviews is to test out some of your hypotheses with those most closely involved. You might, for example, find that some of your superficial views are contradicted entirely by those who are working in the department every day.

It's probably best at this stage not to say too much about your reasons for wishing to conduct the survey, unless these are extremely uncontentious. If you're completely frank, you run a significant risk of influencing responses. If you were to begin by saying to the supervisors, 'Look, Fred, we're very concerned about the high level of absenteeism and turnover in the department. And not only that but productivity's going down as well . . .', then Fred's first reaction will be to cover his own back. He'll begin by telling you everything that's wrong with the workforce, the machinery, his fellow supervisor or the boss . . . You'll have no idea how much of this represents Fred's real views, and how much of it is intended to deflect potential criticism from himself.

On the other hand, if you tell Fred that you're just interested in investigating the views of the workforce on a range of issues and that his department has been selected as a guinea-pig, you may well get a more straightforward approach. In fact, you'll often find that Fred has been waiting for many a long year for the opportunity to give his opinions on the organization.

Of course, this slight economy with the truth does smack of manipulation and may make some feel uneasy. Furthermore, if respondents *do* find out (or even strongly suspect) that you have a hidden agenda, this can severely damage the credibility of the whole exercise. In the end, you'll have to decide for yourself what's appropriate to say to whom. If you don't think you can carry off not telling the whole truth, then don't even try – it'll be much more damaging if you're found out later. You may well also feel that it's unfair to carry out this kind of investigation without explaining your motives fully to all those involved.

Your initial two or three interviews with the relevant managers and supervisors should then be followed up with a representative set of interviews with members of the workforce. In practice, you'll probably need to conduct no more than half a dozen or so of these, either individually or in groups. You're not at this stage trying to construct a statistically valid sample, so you needn't worry unduly about the numbers or composition of the respondents chosen. You're simply trying to get an overall feel for attitudes and opinions across the area you're interested in. However, common sense suggests that you should try to get a reasonably broad spread of individuals. If possible, for instance, you should include individuals at all levels, from the most senior to the most junior. You should also include individuals from all parts of the department, if there are likely to be significant differences between various groups. For example, if one part of the department is in one building and another is elsewhere, then it's obviously sensible to include respondents from both groups – the differences in accommodation could be a significant factor. The same should apply if different parts of the department are engaged in different kinds of work.

Clearly, if the area under scrutiny is very large, it may be difficult to cover all the relevant groups without conducting a very large number of interviews. In such cases, it is usually advisable to make the best of a bad job by covering as broad a range as you can in the small number of interviews available. At this stage, however large the area under scrutiny, it is not generally worth conducting more than a dozen interviews at the outside. Your aims and your methodology are informal, aimed at eliciting a broad range of unstructured information rather than quantifiable or statistically sound data. If you conduct a larger number of interviews, you will generally find that the law of diminishing returns applies – you will not add significantly to the amount of informal data that you would have gathered. You might have begun to confirm and validate some of this data through repetition, but that's not the aim at this point – you can do that much more efficiently through the written questionnaire.

Group discussions

You can, of course, increase the numbers of employees covered in the interviews by making use of group discussions rather than one-to-one interviews. In practice, there are benefits and drawbacks to both approaches. Group discussions enable you to cover a larger number of individuals in one meeting. Moreover, the group dynamic can often be helpful in encouraging open discussion. People relax more quickly and easily when they are among their friends and colleagues, and they can often spark off thoughts and ideas from each other. Once one person breaks the ice by raising some 'difficult' subject – attitudes to the supervisor or criticisms of company policy – others will quickly join in.

On the other hand, group discussions allow you comparatively little time to talk to individuals in depth. It may often be difficult to follow up an intriguing comment in detail because others have moved the conversation on or because the group as a whole is uninterested in the particular issue. And, of course, there's less confidentiality in a group discussion. People may feel reluctant to raise issues which are potentially embarrassing or which they fear might be held against them later.

Individual, one-to-one interviews will help you to overcome some of these problems, and often provide more detailed and personal information. Nonetheless, a one-to-one interview is usually a more formal affair, initially at least, and the interviewer may have to work much harder to develop a relaxed and open atmosphere. And there's always the danger that, if faced with a reticent or nervous interviewee, even a very skilled interviewer may be able to elicit very little information.

For this reason, it's usually best to use both approaches in your preliminary information-gathering. For example, your half-dozen interviews might include, say, four one-to-one interviews and two group discussions. The composition of the groups will depend on the area under scrutiny. On the whole, it is usually preferable to include a range of different respondents in each group, rather than drawing all the members from one grade or work-group. This not only provides you with a broader sample, it also enables you to assess whether there is noticeable consistency or disagreement between the various respondent-groups.

Conducting the interviews

All your interviews – whether they're with managers, supervisors or employees, whether they're one-to-one or in groups – should aim to be as open as possible. They should be perceived as informal discussions, rather than formally structured interviews. You're trying to encourage the general provision of information, not to cross-examine or to produce statistically valid data. Allow the discussion to open out. Don't worry if it strays off the subjects that you expected to talk about. The chances are that you'll find out things you didn't expect to which will have a bearing on your original theories.

In general, it's best to prepare for each interview by drawing up half a dozen or so broad questions. These questions should be open prompts to discussions rather than closed or leading questions. In other words, in the case of the grommet finishers, your questions to the Departmental Manager might include prompts such as 'What's your general view of the relationship between the supervisors and the workforce?' or 'What are your views of the working accommodation?' They should definitely *not* include questions like 'What about old George? Don't you think he's a cantankerous old so-and-so?' or 'Do you think they find this a rather depressing place to work?' Such questions encourage the respondent to say what they think you want to hear. Of course, they might do the same in response to an open question, but at least then they'll have a harder time guessing what you're expecting!

Try to build up a rapport with the interviewees. Encourage a relaxed atmosphere. Don't run methodically through a list of written questions, but treat the meeting as a two-way conversation, even if you do prompt its direction from time to time. If possible, organize the meeting on the respondent's home territory – in his or her office, or at least in the department – rather than summoning them to yours. Try to sit in comfortable chairs with coffee rather than facing each other across a desk crowded with papers. And try to allow plenty of time. This may not be easy, particularly with a busy manager, but it will usually pay dividends. If you allow, say, 1½–2 hours for the interview, this allows the rapport to build up, encourages the respondent to relax and to discover that you don't have a hidden agenda and you're not trying to catch him or her out. Once you've gone through this process, you'll probably find that the interviewee begins to talk much more openly.

The first major rule is: listen! It's all too easy, once you slip happily into conversational mode, to forget to pay attention to what the interviewee is saying. You take in the general import, but you miss out on the important details or the between-the-line hints. For instance, if you're talking to the manager about relationships between supervisors and staff, the manager might say, 'Yes, relationships are pretty good on the whole. I mean, we have our ups and downs – who doesn't? I mean, some of the things old Norman says to the women are a bit near the knuckle, and that can set the fur flying, I can tell you. But no, by and large, we're a happy team, we get on well . . . '

In practice, few managers are going to admit openly to significant problems in their department, in case this reflects on their own performance. On the other hand, unless they're being unusually guarded (that is, unless they have some reason to be suspicious of your motives), they'll probably be reasonably honest overall. The real trick is to pick up the hints, to read between the lines, and take in *all* the information that's provided. In this case, you've got a clue about Norman's behaviour. This may or may not be significant – Norman's comments might range from the odd risqué joke through to downright sexual harassment. But it does give you a clue you can follow up later.

This brings us neatly to the second major rule of these interviews, which is: keep an open mind! Don't prejudge matters or leap to conclusions. This is both prudent and fair. After all, it would be extremely unfair to condemn Norman's behaviour on the basis of one off-the-cuff and unsubstantiated comment. Moreover, such a condemnation would not be helpful to you. If you jump to the conclusion that the department's ills stem from Norman's attitudes to females, you may be simply wrong; even if you're right, you may miss out on other contributory factors. Your role at this stage is not to make judgements, about facts or individuals. Your role is to listen, to take in everything that you hear, and then to identify all those factors which might potentially be significant.

Interpreting your initial findings

Only when you have listened to a range of views will you be able to make any preliminary decisions about which might or might not be worth pursuing. At this stage, you'll be able to assess the range of data you've gathered, and how the various elements weigh up against each other and against your initial theories. Do there appear to be major themes or consistencies which are worth following up? Are there apparent inconsistencies, which also might be worth investigating further? And are there any factors which you can discard as insignificant?

For example, in the case of the grommet finishers, you might find that there are regular and repeated comments about pressure of work and the working accommodation. This supports your preliminary theories and is clearly worth pursuing in more detail. On the other hand, you might find that there are contradictory views about supervisory style. You will then give some thought as to whether this reflects any obvious differences in respondent categories: Are the workforce generally more favourable than management about the supervisors? Does one section of the department seem happier than another? Are men generally happier than women? Clearly, this may well highlight a number of issues that can then be investigated in more detail.

You might also find that there are recurrent themes which did *not* form part of your initial theories. For example, you might find that there are recurrent references to dissatisfaction with a particular unpleasant working practice. As an outsider, you might not even have been aware of this practice, let alone known that it was widely seen as unsatisfactory. If so, you can then add this to your list of theories to be investigated further in the formal survey. Conversely, you might find that there is no reference at all to factors you suspected might be important, even though you prompted reference to them in your questions. For instance, you might find that your prompts about company values or employee attitudes aroused little interest. You might therefore decide to exclude this issue from the formal questionnaire, or to give it a less prominent role than you originally expected.

Summary

- Clarify the specific issues or problems you want the survey to focus on
- Don't assume the obvious cause of problems is the only one – or even the most important
- Use the three-stage 'hourglass' process of preparation, formal survey and follow up
- Draw up a list of preliminary theories you want to test
- Consider the advantages and disadvantages of using consultants at this stage
- Use preliminary interviews and group discussions to explore and extend your initial theories
- Listen carefully and keep an open mind!

Chapter Five

The Written Survey:
1 – Who to Survey?

'For many are called, but few are chosen . . . '

Matthew xxii. 14

After all this preparation, we're finally ready to give some thought to the formal, written part of the survey. About time, too, some readers may be saying. Those who are accustomed to thinking of employee surveys as based on written questionnaires may have been surprised by the time we've taken to get to this point. These readers will probably also be surprised by the things we get up to *after* the written survey's been completed. It's worth reiterating that, while the written survey is usually the pivotal point of the survey process, it should not be the beginning of the process and it should certainly not be the end. After this small caveat, let's move on to look at the issues involved in actually conducting a written survey.

Who conducts the survey?

This chapter, like the rest of this book, is addressed primarily to practising managers, personnel or otherwise. It's not recommended that they should attempt to design or conduct a written survey themselves, unless they already have considerable experience in the area. Even if you have decided to conduct the exploratory interviews, it would almost certainly be prudent to seek the assistance of a third-party expert at this stage.

There are a number of good reasons for this – quite apart from the question of helping to keep me and my colleagues in gainful employment! Firstly, although the skills involved in questionnaire design and administration are much less mystical than you might imagine, they are definitely real and important. We'll discuss some of these skills in the following chapters. However, this book, like any book on this subject, can really only supply the basic materials. Unless you're unusually gifted (or unusually lucky), you'll make significant mistakes in your early attempts at questionnaire design. At best, these might only restrict the amount or usefulness of the data you collect. At worst, you might find that the errors distort the findings, so that you end up making management decisions on an unreliable basis.

Secondly, the issue of confidentiality becomes even more crucial at this stage. As a broad generalization, written surveys have two primary advantages. The first, and most obvious, is that they facilitate the collection of quantifiable data. The second is that, so long as they are anonymous, they encourage the expression of views and attitudes which employees might feel reluctant to reveal verbally. While it's certainly possible to convince employees that interviews are confidential, many will still feel reluctant to express controversial or dissident views in front of others, whoever they might be. Despite all the assurances, they still believe that the information might get back to their bosses.

In general, written questionnaires tend to elicit more honest responses. This is particularly true if the questionnaire is based on multiple-choice selection, so that the respondent doesn't even have to phrase his or her own responses. It's much easier to commit yourself to ticking a box than to formulating your own expressions of criticism or dissident opinion!

However, this is only true so long as the questionnaire is perceived to be truly confidential and anonymous. If the respondent believes that his or her words (or ticks) might be attributable, then there'll be a much greater reluctance to respond honestly. Even if the questionnaire is ostensibly anonymous, many respondents will still feel concerned if it's administered and analysed by internal management. If the questionnaire is sent back to the boss or the local personnel department, there is always a nagging doubt. Employee confidence will be much greater if the survey is administered and analysed by a third-party, who has no detailed knowledge of individual employees. Indeed, I would generally ensure that respondents are able to send the completed questionnaire directly to me, rather than via their line manager or personnel department. In this way, there can be no concern even about inadvertent breaches of confidentiality.

The third benefit of using an external consultant is that it encourages an objective look at your organization and your reasons for wanting to conduct the survey. It's all too easy in this kind of exercise to lose sight of the wood for the trees, especially when you're working in the organization day after day. Often, a third-party can raise issues or ask questions which would be missed by those inside the organization. This may be in comparatively minor respects. For example, the consultant might query whether a question full of in-house jargon is likely to be comprehensible to all employees – what is obvious to managers is not always obvious to those on the shop-floor. Alternatively, an external consultant might raise more major issues by asking questions, for example, about particular working practices which are taken for granted in the organization.

In general, there are very good reasons for employing external help in designing and administering the questionnaire. The only real exceptions to this are those organizations large enough to employ a separate in-house consultancy or organization-development department, which can effectively play the role outlined above. For most organizations, the use of a skilled external consultant is likely to add considerable value to the exercise.

Stay involved!

The use of an external consultant, however, should certainly not mean that you're excluded from the process. The consultant, in designing and administering the questionnaire, will be working to your guidance and your objectives. The better your understanding of the issues involved, the more effectively you will be able to contribute to the process. This should ensure not only that you get maximum value for money from the exercise, but also that the findings of the survey fulfil your management needs and objectives. With this in mind, the following chapters are aimed at providing an understanding of the issues involved in questionnaire design and administration, as well as a basic grounding in the skills needed to conduct a written survey.

The sample of employees

Whatever kind of survey you're conducting, you need to give careful consideration as to whom you're actually going to survey. You then need to consider the implications of this for the accuracy of the findings. Obviously, everything else being equal, the larger the number of people surveyed, the more the results are likely to reflect the views of the overall population. On the other hand, a thoughtlessly constructed large sample will probably be less representative than a thoughtfully constructed small one. A national political opinion poll covering 20% of the population could be very accurate indeed – unless, for example, it was conducted exclusively in the South East of England or in Scotland.

In practice, these questions are usually less critical in an employment context than in, say, political opinion polls or market-research surveys. For the most part, managers will be interested in getting a broad feel for the opinions of the workforce rather than in obtaining absolute accuracy. It doesn't much matter whether it's 75% or 80% of the workforce that opposes relocation – if it's a large majority, then you're going to have difficulties. It doesn't much matter whether it's 15% or 20% of the employees who are happy with the new bonus scheme – either way, it's a pretty small proportion and you're going to have to do something about it. In the end, management is usually a matter of consensus, and you're going to need clear and convincing evidence before you persuade your colleagues to support any action. If, according to your survey, 52% of the workforce supports a particular action and 48% oppose it, the tiny majority is unlikely to sway management decision-making (no matter how accurate the survey), although the virtually equal split between pros and cons may be worth noting.

Nevertheless, this doesn't mean that you can afford to be utterly cavalier with methodology. It simply means that, like the political pollsters and newspaper editors, you need to decide what level of accuracy is acceptable for your purposes. And, in general, because you are likely to be more interested in broad trends than in precise statistics, you can afford to conduct the survey accordingly. But you will still need to take some care. If you want to gain an understanding of the opinions of a particular population – the whole workforce, a particular department or function, or whatever

– you need to ensure that you conduct the survey among a group which is broadly representative of that population.

The first question you need to ask is: how many people are we actually prepared to survey? One of the benefits of employee surveys is that it's sometimes possible to survey the whole population that you're interested in. If you want to find out the opinions of a department of, say, fifty employees, there's no reason why you shouldn't survey all of them, so long as you can afford to do so.

How large a sample can you afford?

If the population is larger, however, you will probably have to give some thought as to what proportion you can realistically survey. This will probably be dictated primarily by cost and time considerations. It will also depend in part on how you decide to conduct the survey. We'll look at the practicalities of surveying in more detail in subsequent chapters, but there are some factors which are peculiar to employee surveys and which are worth considering briefly here.

One advantage of conducting surveys in an employment context is that it's much easier to encourage a full response from the selected sample of respondents. Opinion pollsters, market researchers and other surveyors generally have to assume a partial response – in other words, there will be a significant proportion of the original sample which doesn't respond to the questionnaire. In a postal survey, for example, researchers often obtain a response of only 20–30% even if they encourage responses by offering incentives or sending follow-up requests.

This, in turn, further complicates the issue of sample design. For instance, if the pollster wishes to achieve a final sample size of, say, 200, he or she will need initially to mail the questionnaire to a much larger sample, probably 1,000 or more. Furthermore, the pollster will have to ensure that the process of 'self-selection' – the decision to complete and return the questionnaire – doesn't itself distort the findings. It is notoriously difficult, for example, to obtain 'negative' responses to postal questionnaires, since those with no story to tell tend not to bother replying.

In an employment context, it's much easier to exercise control over survey responses. Rather than simply conducting a postal survey – with employees completing and returning questionnaires in their own time – you can gather together the selected respondents, perhaps in a meeting room or the company canteen. They can be allocated working time to complete the questionnaire, and the forms can be returned at the end. To preserve anonymity, this process can be conducted by a third-party or, in more extreme cases, it could even be carried out off-site.

Clearly, this approach has several advantages. It means that the structure of the final sample can be carefully controlled. It means that responses can be virtually guaranteed from all employees, however apathetic or disaffected (and the responses of these latter groups can often be critical to the success or failure of organizational change!).

However, in return for these benefits, you will need to accept the additional cost of conducting the survey in this way. You will need to be willing to release a significant number of employees for a significant period – probably two hours or more, depending on the size of the questionnaire. You will need to be willing and able to provide (or pay for the use of) suitable accommodation. And you will need to be willing to pay for consultants to conduct and oversee the process. All of these costs will constrain the size of the sample group. In addition, however you conduct the survey, you will also need to take account of the general costs of surveying. These include:

- the costs of printing the questionnaire and other general administration; this is likely to be most significant in a postal survey, where you will need to print and post a large number of questionnaires to obtain a respectable response
- the costs of analysis. In most cases, survey analysis will need to be done by computer and by experts, usually in an appropriately skilled computer bureau. In general, assuming that the questionnaire has been designed to facilitate analysis, the costs of this are comparatively small. Nevertheless, they will increase in proportion to the number of respondents, so this may act as a constraint on sample size.

Having considered these various costs, you can then begin to make a judgement about the numbers of employees that you'll be able to survey. If you are going to conduct the survey during working time, you'll probably also have to reach some agreement with the relevant line managers – and they will often be the biggest constraint of all! No line manager likes to admit that he or she can spare staff even for a minute, let alone the couple of hours or more that this exercise will need.

Some potential pitfalls

Once you've decided how many employees you can afford to cover in the survey, you can then start to select your sample so as to reflect the overall characteristics of the group that you're interested in. Clearly, the larger your sample, the easier it is to make it representative of the overall group. Yet it's difficult to give precise guidance as to how large a sample you'll need (or, more to the point, how small a sample you can get away with). This will depend on a host of factors, including the size, variety and complexity of the total population, the nature of the issues to be covered in the survey, and the level of detail that you require from your findings.

In an employment context, your judgement about sample size might also be influenced by other, more political considerations. For example, if you suspect that there may be significant resistance to the survey findings from senior management, you might decide to reinforce their validity by covering a larger sample. Office politics might also influence the sample selection: if you know that Department X tends to be troublesome, you might decide to survey all members of it. You will then need to adjust the overall sample to ensure that the results are not unduly distorted.

As a very broad rule of thumb, for an employee survey you can probably get away generally with a sample size of around 5–10% of the overall group. This assumes that you are interested in identifying broad trends rather than in producing statistics that are reliable to the percentage point. It also assumes that the group is reasonably homogeneous – clearly, the more disparate the group, the harder it is to construct a representative sample. In addition, before we come to look at sample construction in more detail, it is perhaps worth mentioning two specific problem areas.

The first, and more obvious, problem arises if you want to

obtain the opinions of a very large group of staff – say, over 5,000 employees. In this case, surveying even 5% of the group presents a major challenge, and may well not be affordable. Allowing 250 or more employees working time to complete a survey is not cheap and is likely to incur resistance from line managers. If this is a problem, you will simply have to make a decision. One option is to use a postal survey, perhaps sent out to the whole group initially. With luck, plus some reminders and perhaps even the odd incentive, you may well get a reasonable response – 30% or even higher. On the other hand, you'll have no control over who replies. If the responding sample is not representative, this could distort your figures.

The alternative option is to conduct the survey in working time and merely accept a smaller sample size and its attendant problems. Clearly, if the sample is smaller, it will be harder to make it representative of the total group. On the other hand, at least you'll be able to control the structure to make it as representative as possible, and you'll be aware of the weaknesses of the sample right from the start.

One further option, which is best left to the experts, is to weight the ultimate survey findings to reflect the characteristics of the overall group. To take a very simple example, suppose the total population comprised, say, 75% of Department A and 25% of Department B. You then conduct a postal survey and receive a 20% response. However, only 40% of the responses come from Department A and 60% come from Department B. In this case, you could weight your findings to restore the original proportions – in other words, the responses from Department A would be weighted more heavily than those from Department B. This is a perfectly proper and respectable statistical technique, so long as it is applied competently, and it is often used by professional pollsters to achieve a more representative sample. Nevertheless, it does carry risks, and these risks can be magnified if you are dealing with a comparatively small sample. If, in the example cited here, you had only received replies from 20 members of Department A (out of a possible total of 50), you can't be sure that these 20 are really characteristic of the department as a whole. In a larger sample, you can assume that idiosyncracies will tend to balance out, on a 'swings and roundabouts' basis, but the smaller the sample the greater the scope for distorting the findings.

This also brings us neatly on to the second, less obvious, problem. Just as you may encounter problems trying to conduct a survey across a large population, so you may equally face difficulties covering a small population. Suppose, for instance, that you want to explore the opinions of a department of, say, 50 employees. On the basis of the above rule of thumb, you decide to survey 10% – that is, 5 employees. But how can you tell whether their views are characteristic of the department? How do you know you won't pick five mavericks?

The answer is that you can't tell: you may well pick five individuals whose views *don't* reflect the department as a whole. More to the point, it is arguable that, unless the department is remarkably consistent in its opinions, *no* five employees are likely to be 'typical'. Across a large population, disparate views are likely to balance each other out so that broad trends can be identified. In a group of, say, 5,000, you might well find that there are four or five broad opinions about a given subject. If you survey 500 of the group (or even 250), you will probably find these four or five views reflected in more or less the same proportions. In a group of 50, you will probably encounter the same four or five opinions, but given the size of the group some of these opinions may only be held by three or four people. If you survey only five of the group at random, you may well fail to select *any* who hold these 'minority' views. As a result, your survey may identify only two or three opinions about the subject and so miss out on some crucial issues.

In other words, whatever the size of the original population, if your sample size is too small, your findings may be distorted. If you've surveyed four people out of a department of 40 employees, you can't confidently state that three-quarters of the department would be happy to relocate to Ulan Bator. You may just have stumbled across the three members of the department who've always had a hankering to live in Outer Mongolia. Again, it's difficult to give precise guidance about the minimum acceptable size for a survey sample – it depends very much on the nature of the survey, the issues being investigated, the characteristics of the department, etc. As a *very* rough rule of thumb, though, I'd be suspicious of survey findings based on a sample size smaller than 25, whatever the size of the original population.

Identifying variables

But enough dire warnings. Assuming that you've taken the above advice to heart, how do you then go about trying to construct a sample that is characteristic of the overall group that you want to look at?

First of all, you need to think about the range of variables that are likely to influence employees' opinions about the subject in question. In most cases, three or four primary variables are likely to be most significant in influencing employee opinion – the department or functions that they're working in, the grade and status of their job, their age and possibly their sex. In most of the surveys I've been involved in, these factors have tended to influence the respondents' views more than any other. Of course, the relative importance of the various factors will probably depend on the subject matter of the survey. If you're conducting a survey about, say, retirement age or the pension scheme, age may well be a highly significant factor. Similarly, if you're conducting a survey about, say, introducing a creche or childcare provision, you might well find that opinions tend to be strongly influenced by gender.

In general, though, whatever the focus of the survey, you'll tend to find some noticeable variation across all these categories. For instance, if you're conducting a survey about motivation or employee expectations, you'll very probably find significant differences between junior and senior grades, between different age groups, between different departments and functions, and quite possibly between men and women.

The above categories are likely to be the most relevant, but you may also need to take account of others, depending on the focus of the survey. If you were conducting a survey about a proposed relocation, then responses might well be influenced by factors such as whether respondents are married, whether their spouses have careers, whether they have children of school age, etc. If you feel that these factors are likely to influence responses, you should take account of them in constructing your sample.

Designing the sample

Once you've identified the significant variables, you will then need to analyse the overall group in terms of these variables. For example, let's go back to our grommet finishers. Suppose you've decided that you're going to conduct a survey in the Grommet Finishing Department, which, as luck would have it, happens to comprise some 200 employees. The survey is aimed at exploring the causes of high absenteeism and turnover; you've decided that the relevant variables are likely to be job function, grade, age and gender. You then proceed to analyse the department against these various categories. Firstly, there are four main job functions in the department, as follows:

> Skilled grommet finishers
> Skilled grommet polishers
> Unskilled grommet labourers
> Administrative and support staff.

These categories may be rather arbitrary – for example, they take no account of management staff and may well disregard some smaller groups (such as the two skilled grommet wheelers). There may also be something of an overlap between the grommet finishers and polishers. Nevertheless, your exploratory interviews have led you to believe that these broad divisions are likely to reflect broad variations in opinion. Let's assume that the department's workforce breaks down against these categories as follows:

Skilled grommet finishers	80 employees (40%)
Skilled grommet polishers	60 employees (30%)
Unskilled grommet labourers	30 employees (15%)
Administrative and support staff	30 employees (15%)

In the same way, the department breaks down into four broad grades as follows:

Grade 1	managers and supervisors
Grade 2	skilled staff
Grade 3	semi-skilled/admin. staff
Grade 4	unskilled staff

Again, these divisions are fairly arbitrary. Clearly, you could make more precise divisions, such as splitting managers and supervisors. Nevertheless, your initial interviews and your knowledge of the department suggest to you that these broad bands are likely to reflect significant variations of opinion. In this instance, for example, you feel that managers and supervisors are likely to share broadly the same views. Of course, this will not always be the case – in a different department or with different issues under consideration, there might well be a significant split between managers and supervisors. Again, let's assume that the department's workforce breaks down against these grades as follows:

Grade 1	15 employees (7.5%)
Grade 2	130 employees (65%)
Grade 3	25 employees (12.5%)
Grade 4	30 employees (15%)

Astute readers may have already spotted a problem – and a very significant one, as it turns out. The problem is simply this: the different variables we've identified are not necessarily independent. In this case, there are some fairly straightforward correlations between respective categories. For example, it's clear that the category of unskilled grommet labourers almost certainly comprises exactly the same employees as Grade 4. Similarly, if slightly less neatly, the group of administrative/support staff correlates pretty closely with Grade 3. And so on.

In practice, as far as employee surveys are concerned, these correlations between different variables will not usually affect *the construction of the sample*. Indeed, they probably make life slightly easier, in that they reduce the number of independent variables that you have to take account of.

However, these correlations will be extremely important when you come *to interpret the data*. For this reason, it's as well to be aware of them from the start – in other words, when you're actually putting the sample together. Then you won't miss some important link or relationship between the variables which might affect your analysis. Often the correlations will be more complex and less obvious than those above. I was recently involved in a survey on attitudes to pay, conducted in an organization where the majority of female employees were concentrated in lower-grade jobs. The survey findings were broken down in a variety of ways, such as by grade, department and gender. 'Look!' said one of the managers. 'Isn't that just typical! The women tend to be dissatisfied with their pay, whereas the men are much more contented. I always knew that women were more ambitious!' Of course, the manager had ignored the fact that, because of the high correlation between the two variables of gender and grade, the men were probably happier because on average they earned twice as much as the women!

We'll come back to these issues when we look in more detail at approaches to interpretation. However, it's worth giving some thought to the interdependence of variables while you're actually analysing the original population and constructing your sample. In this way, you're more likely to be aware of the less obvious correlations between variables: Do members of a particular department or grade tend to be younger than others? Does a particular department tend to employ women?

With this in mind, you continue your analysis of the composition of the overall population against the remaining variables. Just as we have analysed the Grommet Finishing Department by job-type and by grade, so you would by age and gender. Analysis by gender is usually straightforward (most people can only be categorized in one of two ways), but analysis by age may be more complex. As with job-type and grade, you'll need to decide which age ranges are likely to be relevant in terms of influencing opinion. You might, for example, decide that three broad age bands are likely to be relevant – say, 18–30, 31–50 and 51–65 – since these are likely to reflect different expectations of work, career and reward. On the other hand, you might sometimes find that it is worth distinguishing, say, 60–65 year-olds as a separate category, since this group is likely to hold different views about retirement or the pension scheme.

Once you've carried out these analyses, you will have a detailed breakdown of the overall population – in this case, the Grommet Finishing Department – against the different variables. On this basis, you can then begin to construct the sample to be surveyed so that it reflects similar proportions of the different variables. In the case of the grommet finishers, for example, suppose you'd decided to take a sample of 40 (20% of total). This should be large enough, both in absolute terms and in relation to the overall population. You would then select a sample so that it contained similar proportions of each variable as the full population – that is, similar proportions of each grade, job-type, age group and gender.

In this case, particularly as a number of the variables are inter-dependent, you would have no problem constructing a sample which closely reflects these proportions. However, if the sample is comparatively small in relation to the overall group, you might find that it is not able to accommodate all the variables accurately. If you do run into problems of this kind, you will need to prioritize the variables you've identified. In other words, you will need to decide which are likely to be most relevant, given the subject-matter of the survey. You might, for example, decide that opinions are likely to vary most according to grade, and that the age or job-type is comparatively unimportant. In this case, you would take care to ensure that your sample is representative in terms of grade, even if this distorted the proportions of other variables.

Summary

- Questionnaire design is a technical skill requiring knowledge and experience
- External consultants can often provide the necessary expertise, confidentiality and objectivity, but always stay involved!
- Protect the anonymity of respondents
- Decide how large you can afford to make your sample, but do not make it too small!
- Select your sample so that it reflects the whole population in terms of variables like age, sex, grade and department
- Aim to obtain a clear picture of the broad trends rather than precise measurements.

Chapter Six

The Written Survey
2 – Designing the Questionnaire

'Them that asks no questions isn't told a lie . . . '

Kipling, 'A Smuggler's Song'

Now that you've decided *who* you're going to survey, you're finally ready to start thinking about *how* you're going to do it. In my experience, this is the point at which you're most likely to run into trouble. The exact nature of the trouble will probably depend on whether you've bravely elected to carry out the survey yourself or prudently commissioned someone else to do the job on your behalf. In the first case, you'll probably find that everyone blames you for not asking the right questions or focussing on the right issues. In the second case, you'll probably just find that everyone blames you for wasting the organization's money on people who won't ask the right questions or focus on the right issues!

Most books on questionnaire design tend to focus on the technicalities of formulating questions and designing the form. These are important issues, of course, and I recommend one or two useful books on page 161 for those who want to pursue this further. But in an employment context these technicalities are often only a secondary course of concern. The primary problems arise at a more basic level – usually with the sheer practicalities of getting the questionnaire written and agreed. Before we come on to the more sophisticated aspects of questionnaire design, let's just take a few moments to define some basic ground rules.

Too many cooks . . .

The first ground rule is: *never let the questionnaire be designed by a committee*. We all know the old joke about a camel being a horse designed by a committee. Personally, I've always thought that the camel was too practical an animal ever to have emerged from the deliberations of a committee. Most of the committees I've ever been involved with would probably have come up with a cross between a dodo and a giant panda. Certainly, a survey questionnaire designed by a committee is often a total mess.

This isn't to say that you shouldn't involve others in the questionnaire-design process. We've already discussed the importance of obtaining commitment. And if you're going to obtain commitment, you'll almost certainly have to involve a wide range of individuals in the design and administration of the survey. In general, people are much happier to support an exercise if they feel that their views have been taken into account.

But while this involvement is important, it's equally important that you (or whoever's ultimately responsible for designing the questionnaire) retain final control. In the end, questionnaire design is a 'one-person' job – a single individual should be responsible for deciding how to formulate questions, which issues to cover, which questions to ask and which to discard.

If you fail to maintain this control, you'll almost certainly find that the questionnaire turns into a mish-mash of confused content and uncertain purpose. This advice is based on bitter experience. I've watched too many committees pulling apart questionnaires, with a dozen people insisting on inserting their two penn'orth and trying to exclude everyone else's. I've spent far too long in these situations trying to please everyone and usually ending up with a questionnaire which pleases no one, least of all me. At worst, these meetings can turn into rather unpleasant political battles, with the original aims of the survey lost beneath the deafening sound of managers grinding axes. But even at best, if everyone is basically well-meaning, the intended focus of the survey can easily get lost.

There are a whole host of danger signals to look out for at this point. Usually, they begin with phrases like 'I think the questionnaire's jolly good. But it does seem to me that while we're at it we might as well ask a few questions about . . . ' or 'Yes, this is well and good, but I'm a bit surprised that we haven't broadened the subject to include . . . ' Those who've never been involved in conducting a survey tend to assume that questionnaires are more or less infinitely expandable.

It's often difficult to resist this kind of pressure, especially when managers begin to play cards like, 'Look, this survey's costing us umpteen thousand pounds. I think the least you can do is make sure that it asks *all* the right questions . . . ' But you *must* resist it.

What's the aim of the survey, anyway?

This brings us to the second golden rule. I have made the point several times already, but since it's usually one of the crucial factors in a successful survey, it bears repetition. The rule is simply this: *before you start to design the questionnaire, make sure you're clear in your mind what the survey is trying to achieve.* And, perhaps more to the point, make sure that everyone else understands as well.

It's surprising how often managers begin to embark on the process of questionnaire design with still only a fairly hazy notion of what they're actually setting out to do. By the time you start designing the questionnaire, assuming you've followed the advice in the previous chapters, you should generally have identified no more than half a dozen primary issues that you want to investigate through the formal survey. Of course, pollsters can and do conduct surveys looking at many more issues than this. Yet if the survey is to form the basis for practical management actions and decisions, you really need to focus your information gathering very specifically. Most managers, especially when using surveys for the first time, feel that they should cover all possible angles, in case they should miss some significant issue or cause.

The problem with this approach is that you can easily end up with a mass of fairly useless, and even contradictory, information. At the same time, you'll have insufficient detail about the issues that are really important. If you're investigating a problem of, say, high labour turnover in a particular department, you might feel that you need to consider everything from supervisory style through issues of job satisfaction to questions of pay and reward.

Quite probably, your findings will suggest that each of these is important to some members of the department. But if the questionnaire covers a very wide range of such issues, your survey will accommodate only very broad findings on each of them. All too often this leaves senior managers saying, 'Well yes, this is all very interesting. I can see that there's room for action here. And here. And here. Oh, and here. But what should we actually *do*?' If you're not careful, you're back at square one.

To avoid these problems, you should reduce your options once you've completed your exploratory interviews. By all means start off with a very wide range of possible issues, if you're not sure which are the important ones, but use the interviewing process to identify the ones that really matter. In most cases, you should find that your original list is quickly reduced to the small number of issues that crop up over and over again or the ones that inspire the most vehement reactions.

In an ideal world – or if you were conducting a more academic form of research – it might be preferable to explore all the issues. It might be interesting to find out, for example, whether or not management style had any impact on turnover. But an employee survey can't really afford to accommodate these 'nice to knows'. The whole purpose of this kind of survey is, quite simply, *to support future management decisions and actions*, nothing more and nothing less. And let's face it, unless you happen to work in a very unusual organization, it's very unlikely that more than three or four major changes or decisions will be taken as a result of the survey. Even then, management will probably demand very clear evidence that they're doing the right thing.

What do you need to know?

Now that you've identified the small number of issues that you're going to investigate, you're ready to start putting together the questions. This brings us to the third golden rule, which is this: *make sure that the questionnaire is going to provide all the detail you need*. In other words, make sure you ask all the questions you need to ask and make sure you ask them precisely and unequivocally. It is all too common to see survey results which say, '85% of those surveyed are unhappy with the bonus scheme' or '75%

of those surveyed expressed discontent with the management style of the organization.'

Well yes, you think, that's interesting. But *why* exactly are they unhappy with the bonus scheme? *What* is it about the management style that they don't like? And – more to the point – what are we supposed to do about it? If you're lucky the survey findings might give you a few hints: '65% of people thought the bonus was too low' or '57% thought that the management style was too "autocratic".'

That's a little more helpful. At least, we know what particular aspects people are unhappy with. But it doesn't really help us decide what to do next. After all, it's hardly a surprise that people think the bonus is too low – people don't usually claim that they're overpaid, at least not to their bosses. And, yes, people think that management is too autocratic. But what does that mean? Which management? All managers, or just a few individuals? And autocratic in what way? Does this refer to some specific way of behaving or simply to their general attitude?

Of course, this is an exaggeration. But not by much. I've seen countless questionnaires which have simply failed to get down to the nitty-gritty of what management really needs to know. It is very easy to frame very broad, general questions. It is much harder to frame the very precise questions that will help you explore the issues in detail. Indeed, managers are sometimes nervous of asking such questions because they feel that they're getting a little close to the bone. If you ask a general question, then people can give nice general answers.

Structuring the questions

In practice, unless the answers are specific, they're not likely to be much use to you. You need to know where the problems lie, what remedial action you can take, what changes will improve things. Inevitably that will sometimes involve implicit or explicit criticism of particular individuals. But if there are problems, you need to be aware of them so that you can start taking steps to put them right.

So, in the example given above, you would probably need to follow up the general questions about the bonus scheme or management style with some much more specific probing questions such as: 'What aspects of the bonus scheme do you find particularly satisfactory/unsatisfactory?', 'In what ways do you think the bonus scheme might be improved?', 'What kinds of behaviour do you think are characteristic of the organization's management approach?', 'What kinds of management behaviour do you find particularly satisfactory/unsatisfactory?' etc.

This process is really a kind of formalized version of the technique that many of us are already accustomed to using verbally in, for example, selection interviews. You begin by asking a general, *open* question, which tries to avoid leading the respondent or implying any judgement on the issue. You probe more deeply by asking either for a more precise definition or for evidence or examples to back up the case. You might then follow that up still further by checking or confirming some of the apparent views that have been expressed.

This process is comparatively straightforward in verbal interviews, which are interactive, but in a written questionnaire it is more problematic. You have to design the questions, with no definite idea of how the respondent will reply, in ways which enable you to obtain detailed responses in any case.

In practice, though, this process isn't usually too difficult. One simple approach is to begin by asking an open question, with a fairly wide range of possible responses. For example, you might ask:

Which words to you think best describe the management style of the organization? [tick no more than 3]

participative	[ ]
autocratic	[ ]
friendly	[ ]
decisive	[ ]
formal	[ ]
etc.	

This kind of open question is often useful in helping to clarify the respondent's overall views about the subject under consideration. It provides you with a context in which to consider his or her subsequent responses, and it provides the respondent with an opportunity to sit back briefly and think, 'Well yes, what *do* I really think of this outfit?' If you proceed too quickly into more detailed or specific questions, you'll sometimes find that the respondent gives an ill-considered response, just regurgitating 'knee jerk' coffee-time opinions: 'Well, of course management are just a bunch of idiots, we all know that . . . ' By contrast, a wide-ranging question like this, which doesn't offer just a straight 'yes or no' choice, will encourage the respondent to think, 'I know I don't think much of management, but why is that? How would I describe them exactly?'

You'll notice that the range of options is pretty diverse and tends to avoid straightforward opposites (not 'formal' and 'informal', for instance, but 'formal' and 'friendly'). This makes it harder for the respondent simply to plump for all negative (or indeed all positive) responses automatically. Similarly, you might include near-synonyms, with positive and negative overtones – for example, 'autocratic' and 'authoritative'. In addition, it's a good idea to scatter the options fairly randomly, rather than offering all the negative options followed by all the positive ones or alternating positive and negative. The overall intention is to encourage the respondent to stop for a moment before making the selection. The restriction to 'less than three' is also helpful. If the respondent is going to tick all negative options, at least he or she will have to spend a moment deciding which ones to choose!

It's often a good idea to follow up this kind of broad opening gambit with a more precise question aimed at identifying the respondent's *evaluation* of the subject. It's all too easy to misinterpret answers: you might think that the respondent has picked entirely negative options, whereas he or she might think the selections are very favourable! Personally, I'm not all that keen on an autocratic, formal, unfriendly management style, but some people think, probably reasonably, that this is what management should be all about. To avoid these kinds of misunderstandings, it's worth asking a straightforward follow-up question, such as:

What is your overall opinion of the organization's management?

very favourable	[	]
fairly favourable	[	]
fairly unfavourable	[	]
very unfavourable	[	]

This should give you a pretty direct idea of where you stand! Once you've got this information, you can then proceed to ask a series of more specific questions. The precise direction and form of these questions will depend on the information that you're trying to elicit. You might, for example, ask questions about different aspects of management activity, such as:

How well do you think your manager fulfils the following aspects of his/her job? [delete as applicable]

decision-making	well/badly
person management	well/badly
leadership	well/badly
finance/resource management	well/badly
etc.	

In short, you're trying to obtain information which is sufficiently detailed and specific for you to take action in response. At the end of the sequence of questions, you should be in a position to make judgements like, 'Well, we've obviously got a major problem with the management style of the organization. It's generally viewed in an unfavourable light. Most people seem to think that it's unfriendly, overly formal and autocratic. The most serious problems seem to be in the area of general person management. At the same time, a lot of employees seem to think that we've got a problem with our approach to leadership. And, on top of that, despite being autocratic, we're also seen as incapable of making decisions . . . ' And so on.

To avoid the process becoming too negative, you might also include some questions seeking the respondent's views about what could be done to improve the situation. You might, for example, ask something like:

What changes do you think would be most likely to improve your manager's effectiveness as a leader? [tick no more than 3]

more willingness to listen	[ ]
greater decisiveness	[ ]
more effective communication of decisions	[ ]

more informal contacts between all
members of the department   [   ]
ect

This kind of question should again assist you in making appropriate changes. If, for example, a large majority of your respondents think their managers' leadership ability would be improved
by better informal communications, then you can think about the
introduction of mechanisms to achieve this – briefing groups,
lunchtime meetings in the pub, or whatever.

One final point – don't ask your respondents questions unless
you're reasonably sure they can give you a meaningful answer.
This might seem painfully obvious, but a few examples will show
how easy it is to overlook. I've seen questionnaires which asked,
for instance:

What information would you like to be given that's not currently being provided?

A reasonable reply to this question would be: 'How should I
know?' Respondents might conceivably be aware of interesting
information that's not formally communicated, but there could be
a whole mass of data that they have never even heard about. This
is a problem often encountered in surveys on communications –
people don't know what they don't know. In this case, you'd have
to give respondents some idea of the possible options – financial
information, data on business strategy, etc. – before asking them
to give an opinion.

I've also seen questionnaires which asked:

Do you think most managers in the organization do a good
job?

Again, a reasonable response would be: 'Search me! I can only
tell you about the bloke I work for – I suppose I could give you
a view about some of the others, but it'd only be based on hear-
say.' There are two dangers with this kind of question. The first
is that respondents might simply be baffled by it and so leave it
blank. In that case, you'll be failing to obtain potentially valuable
information. The bigger danger is that the respondent will attempt

to answer the question, on the basis of incomplete or inaccurate knowledge. In this case, you'll be obtaining information all right – but it could be highly misleading.

Wording the questions

Before we move on to consider other aspects of questionnaire structure and design, this is probably a good moment to give some thought to the actual wording of questions. Let's start with the basics. In most questionnaires, the majority of your questions are going to be multiple- or forced-choice questions.

There are two primary reasons for using such questions, one better than the other. The first – and better – reason is to make the questionnaire as easy as possible to complete. Ideally, you want to ensure that the questionnaire can be completed in a very short time (probably no more than an hour at the outside, unless you've got *very* good reasons for making it longer), and with a minimum of intellectual and physical effort. This doesn't mean that you don't want your respondents to think about their answers – as we've seen in the examples above, it's quite possible to design multiple-choice questions which encourage respondents to think before they tick. But you want respondents' intellectual efforts to go into selecting the most appropriate answer rather than into framing an elegant response.

The second, slightly less good, reason for using multiple-choice questions is that, in conducting a written questionnaire, you're at least in part trying to obtain *quantifiable* information. In other words, you want to be able to say, afterwards, that 45% of respondents thought such-and-such and 57% thought something else. If you don't use multiple-choice questions you might find yourself faced with two hundred different responses, which would then have to be crudely reduced into broad categories for analytical purposes. By using multiple-choice questions, you are predetermining the categories so that respondents have to choose between them.

Any other comments?

Some readers may wonder why I describe this as a 'less good' reason. After all, if you're conducting formal research, surely it's essential that you can produce detailed and reliable statistical results? Well, yes and no. If you're conducting a market survey, a political opinion poll or many other kinds of formal research, statistical results are obviously paramount. This is probably also true if you're conducting an employee survey amongst a very large population. If you're investigating opinion in an organization of 20,000 employees, then you obviously need a shorthand means of identifying trends. There's no point in saying, 'Jim Smith in Accounts thinks this, but Alan Robinson in Marketing thinks that. On the other hand, Bill Johnson in Production says that . . . ' You need to be able to say, for example, that 25% hold one view, while 37% think the opposite.

But it's worth remembering that many employee surveys will be carried out among much smaller populations than this. The techniques we've been describing are appropriate not only for huge multinationals, but also for much smaller organizations or for one or two departments in a larger organization. If you're going to relocate your fifty-strong advertising department down the road, there's no reason why you shouldn't conduct a survey to investigate their opinions about the move.

If you are carrying out a survey amongst a comparatively small population, you may well find that the non-statistical, narrative data obtained is more important than the statistical data. The fact that 20% of the group is unhappy with the move may be neither here nor there. What's much more important is the fact that three people are concerned about problems with their children's education or that two have to look after aging relatives. In other words, the same old golden rule once again applies: *the important information is that which will improve your decision-making.* If that information happens to be obtained in the 'any other comments' section of the survey rather than from the statistical data, so be it.

The point is worth making, because it's easy – whether you're an experienced researcher or a novice – to get overly concerned about the statistical elements of an employee survey and to miss valuable data which is coming from other, less structured parts of the questionnaire. So, to return to where we started, the majority of your questions will be multiple-choice – but some should not be. All questionnaires should allow the respondent some space, if only at the end, to make additional comments.

While it's certainly important for you to know what the overall workforce thinks, in the end you have to deal with individuals. And the more information you can gather about individuals the better at this stage. To achieve this, it's often a good idea to include an 'other comments' section at regular stages in the questionnaire. This might be at the end of each section or even – and I've seen this done to good effect – after each question. In the latter case, you would have a small space after the range of multiple-choice answers for narrative comment, thus:

What is your overall opinion of the organization's management?

highly favourable	[ ]
fairly favourable	[ ]
fairly unfavourable	[ ]
highly unfavourable	[ ]
other comments.................	

In this way, you're encouraging respondents to include their comments as they think of them. If they have to wait till the end of the form, it's quite likely that passing, but perhaps important, thoughts may be forgotten.

Forcing the choice

On the whole, though, despite the above caveats, you'll want to formulate the majority of your questions as multiple-choice. This is often quite a skill in itself. It's much easier simply to ask an open question than to offer a predetermined range of options. In particular, you need to be careful to offer meaningful options and to include all the options that are likely to be popular. I've come across one or two cases where questionnaire designers have omitted such options, leading to headaches at the analysis stage.

Suppose, for example, you were asking a question about motivation, along the following lines:

Which of these factors most motivates you in your work? [tick one only]

your own satisfaction in doing a good job	[ ]
recognition of your work by colleagues	[ ]
recognition of your work by your boss	[ ]
the prospect of promotion	[ ]
some other factor [please specify]	[ ]

If, having read your Herzberg, you'd decided not to include salary as a motivator, you might still find an awful lot of people ticking the 'other factor' box. If other respondents felt motivated by different kinds of financial reward – the bonus or incentive scheme, for instance – you might find that some would tick the final box on this basis as well. When you calculated the responses (or, more commonly, when you received the results back from the software house), they might well read:

your own satisfaction in doing a good job	15%
recognition of your work by colleagues	12%
recognition of your work by your boss	10%
the prospect of promotion	15%
some other factor	48%

You would then have the task of going through all the narrative data contained in the 'please specify' section to identify the proportions motivated by salary, by the bonus scheme, and by a variety of other factors. If you're dealing with a large response, this will be a time-consuming task. Furthermore, if a large proportion of your respondents have cited simply 'money' as the prime motivator, you don't know whether they're motivated more by the salary or by the bonus scheme. If you want to take management action to improve motivation, this could be an important distinction.

It's surprisingly easy to omit an important option, even when the questionnaire has been scrutinized by a number of interested parties. Your exploratory interviews should be helpful in identifying the most relevant options, but they may well have to be supplemented by some careful thought. If that fails, you can still hope to pick up any significant omissions during the pilot stage (which we'll come on to in the next chapter).

Before we leave the subject of multiple-choice, it's perhaps worth discussing a couple of further issues. The first, following on from the example above, is whether or not you should include an 'other' option for each question. When should respondents be allowed to ignore the options you've provided and provide some option of their own?

Basically, it depends on the extent to which you want to force the respondent to plump for a predetermined option. And this in turn will depend on the nature of the question. It's usually appropriate to offer an 'other' option if, as in the above question on motivation, there are a wide range of possible responses and you're simply unable to include all of them. After all, you want to find out what really motivates respondents, and you wouldn't want to exclude an answer just because you hadn't included it in the predetermined list. If the respondent happened to be motivated by, say, the sheer pleasure of operating a grommet-finishing machine, then you'd want to know this. If there were no 'other' option, the respondent – unless he or she had the presence of mind to ignore your options – might feel obliged to plump for a secondary motivator, and you would fail to obtain a potentially valuable piece of information.

On the other hand, there will also be occasions when you *do* wish to force respondents to plump for one of your predetermined options. Most commonly, this will be in questions where you want to force the respondent off the fence – for example, in questions where you're offering a spectrum of possible value-judgements. Suppose, for instance, you were to ask:

Overall, how much do you like your job?

very much indeed	[ ]
quite a lot	[ ]
not very much	[ ]
not at all	[ ]

Left to ourselves, most of us would probably equivocate in

response to this kind of question: 'Well, it depends what you mean by "like". I mean, sometimes I like it, and other times I find it a pain in the backside. It depends what kind of work we're doing that day, what sort of mood the boss is in . . . and what sort of mood *I'm* in!'

This kind of response may be honest, but it's not a lot of use to the person who's trying to get an overall picture. You want a broad overview of people's attitudes, not a complex account of how much their attitudes are affected, day to day, by a host of factors. To achieve this, you don't offer the respondent an opportunity to provide these details, just as you don't offer the respondent the opportunity to respond 'Sometimes I like it and sometimes I don't.' Instead, you force the respondent to weigh up his or her views and to opt – by and large, and all things considered – for a positive or a negative response.

Multiple-choice bias?

This brings us to the second point about multiple-choice questions – the issue of bias. There has been some concern over the years about whether the use of multiple-choice questions might itself introduce an element of bias into the survey. Is there, for example, any evidence that respondents tend to plump more frequently for any particular option – the first, the last or any in between?

Considerable research has been carried out in this area, but it has proved largely inconclusive. For the purposes of employee surveys it's probably not worth worrying too much about it. However, one factor is worth bearing in mind. There is evidence that, if you offer respondents an odd number of options, they'll display an excessive tendency to plump for the middle one. This is particularly true if the options represent a scale of values. People don't like to commit themselves to 'extreme' views, so they tend to opt for the safe middle ground. To avoid possible bias, it's a good idea to offer an even number of options wherever possible.

Let's now move on to some more general issues that you'll need to consider in wording the questions. It's difficult to offer too many generalizations, but there are a few broad guidelines that you can bear in mind in formulating your questions.

Leading questions

The first guideline is *to avoid leading questions*. We've already
mentioned the possible bias that can arise in the use of multiple-
choice questions, but there is a far greater danger that your findings will be distorted by leading or biased wording. We all know
that it's not difficult to introduce deliberate bias into political
opinion polls or market-research surveys. Indeed, if you're dealing
with highly complex issues, as so often in politics, it's sometimes
hard to tell where bias begins. For example, is it fairer to ask:

> Would you be prepared to pay higher taxes to achieve better
> public services?

than to ask simply:

> Would you like better public services?

The answer is, of course, that neither question is entirely fair.
The first begs a number of questions: Is there a necessary link
between better services and higher taxes? Would the respondent
prefer tax revenue to be spent on services rather than on, say,
defence? And so on. On the other hand, the second is a rather
unhelpful question of the 'Do you approve of motherhood?'
variety. Of course, all else being equal, most of us would like
better public services. The more important question is whether
we'd be prepared to accept the attendant costs or the reductions
in other areas of public spending. If you were trying to conduct
unbiased research into this area, you would have to word your
questions much more carefully.

In employee surveys, deliberate bias should not normally be a
problem. However, I have occasionally come across situations
where managers have wanted to bias questions to avoid producing
unwelcome findings: 'Look, I know we're asking them what they
most dislike about the organization. But we can't include the
Managing Director as one of the options, because they'll all plump
for that . . . '! I've even once or twice encountered managers who
want to use surveys primarily for purposes of internal PR: 'We've
got to get a positive response from this survey. Morale's bad

enough as it is. We're hoping that this is going to perk it up a bit!'

In Machiavellian terms, this may or may not be legitimate practice. But it certainly isn't a legitimate employee survey. The purpose of a survey is to obtain information. If you've already made up your mind what you want to hear, then you might as well not bother.

Even if deliberate bias isn't a problem, unintentional bias often is. It's all too easy to bias the wording of a question without meaning to – most often simply from an unfortunate choice of words. For example, suppose you asked:

Do you find your work challenging and fulfilling?

This is intended as a neutral question. But the choice of words could be taken, particularly by a nervous or insecure respondent, as implying that the questionnaire is ideally looking for a positive rather than a negative response. On this basis, a borderline respondent might easily be led to give a positive answer, even if this didn't accurately represent his or her views. A better wording might therefore have been:

What is your opinion of your work?

In short, you should try to avoid any wording which might, however remotely, be perceived as implying a value-judgement. Always remember that, however good your preparation, some respondents wil be feeling nervous, some will be suspicious of your motives in conducting the survey, some will worry that you're trying to catch them out, and so on. In this context, some of them will seize upon any clue or hint, however tenuous, that you want them to respond in a particular way. If you're in any doubt at all about whether your wording could imply a bias, err on the side of caution.

Ambiguity

Just as you should be scrupulous in avoiding bias, so you should also take considerable care to avoid ambiguity in wording your questions. This may seem an obvious point, but it's remarkably easy to introduce unintentional and unnoticed ambiguities into questions. And, again, nervous or tense respondents often have an astonishing talent for detecting ambiguities which would have gone unnoticed by the rest of mankind! If there are two possible ends of a stick, you can bet that at least some respondents will grab the wrong one.

As an example of this, I once saw a research questionnaire, intended to investigate various aspects of retirement, which had been sent out to a sample of UK organizations. It included this question:

> Over the past 12 months, what percentage of your employees have retired below the age of 60 with a company pension?

In asking this question, the researchers simply wanted to know how many employees had taken early retirement. When the responses came back, the researchers found that a significant proportion had given the answer '100%' to this question. For a while, they were baffled. Was it really true that, in a significant proportion of UK companies, *all* the employees were retiring before the age of 60? Eventually, they realized what had happened. Those respondents who had given the answer '100%' had misinterpreted the question. They had assumed that it meant:

> Of those staff who have retired below the age of 60 over the past 12 months, what proportion have received a company pension?

In many companies, of course, the answer was that all of them had.

As this example demonstrates, you have to take care to avoid not only actual ambiguity, but also the possibility of respondents misreading or misinterpreting the question. This is particularly important if you're presenting a complex question or one which includes terms which might be unfamiliar to respondents.

For the same reason, you should endeavour to make your questions as clear as possible. Don't make assumptions about what your respondents will know. Just because you know the ins and outs of the company bonus scheme, don't assume that all the other employees do. Some may only know the basic principles of the scheme, and a few may not even know those. Similarly, don't use technical terms if you can possibly avoid it. If you have to use such terms, then make sure that you explain them.

Structure and layout

A well-designed layout can often be helpful in clarifying the questionnaire and avoiding confusion. If the respondent has to cope with tiny, badly photocopied typescript, then it's much more likely that he or she will misread questions. On the other hand, if the form is well laid out with bold print, then you're much more likely to avoid misinterpretation. You'll also need to consider how you will analyze the survey results. If you intend to analyze the results by computer, you'll need to design the questionnaire with this in mind. This is discussed in more detail on page 120.

For the same reason, it's also a good idea to make the structure of the form as straightforward as possible. Many questionnaire designers use complex instructions to ensure that respondents don't fill in superfluous questions. The respondent might be told:

If you answered 'yes' to Question 7, go to Question 14. If you answered 'no', continue with Question 8.

This kind of instruction can sometimes be a helpful mechanism for providing appropriate follow-up questions to the respondent's initial answer. However, it's best not to overuse this device. It can be confusing, especially if the questionnaire then starts leading the respondent into further sub-sections. I've occasionally known respondents misunderstand or misread such instructions, with the result that they failed to complete a necessary part of the questionnaire. Even if this is avoided, you may find that respondents are concentrating so hard on the instructions that they don't think properly about their responses.

Incidentally, if the questionnaire runs to several pages, do remember to number the pages clearly. We've all witnessed examinees turning over two pages at once and automatically losing 30% of their possible marks. This happens just as frequently in the completion of questionnaires, but then it's the surveyor rather than the respondent who loses out. Large, clear numbering, ideally placed in the top right-hand corner where it can't be missed, should help minimize this risk.

Lies, damned lies . . .

Let's finish our review of questionnaire design by going back to the epigram from Kipling that began the chapter. Up to now we've been assuming that respondents will answer your questions honestly. But do people generally respond honestly? And, if they don't, what can you do about it?

The short answer is that, by and large, people do respond honestly to employee surveys so long as you've prepared the ground properly beforehand. In the next chapter, we'll look in more detail at the implementation of the formal survey. We'll examine not only how you should actually administer the question-naire, but also how you should introduce it beforehand.

Yet even if you do take appropriate care in preparing for the survey, some questions may still tend to encourage dishonest responses. This occurs most often when respondents stand to gain personally from a particular response. Suppose, for example, that you are trying to find out whether employees are generally satis-fied or dissatisfied with various elements of organizational prac-tice. You have formulated a series of questions, as follows:

What are your opinions about office accommodation?

generally very satisfied	[ ]
generally fairly satisfied	[ ]
generally fairly dissatisfied	[ ]
generally very dissatisfied	[ ]

On the whole, people will probably respond reasonably honestly to this kind of question. Most respondents won't, for example, express major dissatisfaction about the office accommodation unless they really feel it. At least, this is true until one reaches a question such as:

What are your opinions about the level of your salary?

generally very satisfied	[ ]
generally fairly satisfied	[ ]
generally fairly dissatisfied	[ ]
generally very dissatisfied	[ ]

In this case, many respondents may feel that they have something to gain by expressing dissatisfaction. After all, who is ever fully satisfied with the level of his or her salary? It's always worth claiming to be dissatisfied, on the off-chance that management might add a bit more to next year's pay deal.

You might well find that, say, 75% of respondents claim to be unhappy with their salary. But what does this mean? Is it a real problem, which requires that you take action, or is it simply a piece of mild opportunism? At the analysis stage, there's no real way of knowing. However, with a little care, you can design the questionnaire so that it gives you a more detailed insight into respondents' overall attitudes. This in turn should provide some indications of how seriously you need to take this particular response.

The simplest way of achieving this is a process which is sometimes known as *funnelling*. You begin by asking broad, general questions, and then gradually 'funnel' down to ask more specific, detailed questions. The initial questions then provide a context within which to evaluate the more specific questions. In the above case, for example, you might begin by asking:

Which aspects of organizational practice do you find most unsatisfactory? [tick no more than three]

management/supervisory style	[ ]
promotion prospects	[ ]
production methods	[ ]
salary	[ ]
etc.	

If only 15% cite salary as a major source of dissatisfaction, then this suggests that, whatever the response to the more specific question, it is not a primary cause for concern. In short, the general question provides a mechanism for validating the more specific responses obtained elsewhere in the survey. While this doesn't guarantee that respondents will be fully honest, it does at least provide a basis for meaningful evaluation. And that, as we'll see shortly, is often the key to an effective survey.

Summary

- Never let a committee design a questionnaire!
- Keep the aim of the survey firmly in mind throughout
- Try and obtain as much detail as you need
- Use open general questions and then 'funnel' down to probe more deeply
- Multiple-choice questions force employees to respond and provide quantifiable information
- Avoid leading questions, bias and ambiguity.

Chapter Seven

The Written Survey
3 – How to Administer the Questionnaire

' . . . Suit the action to the word, the word to the action . . . '

Hamlet III. ii. 20

You have finished preparing a carefully designed questionnaire which explores thoroughly all the questions you're interested in. You feel reasonably confident that it will provide you with enough detailed information for your purposes. Now, you think, you're ready to try it out on real respondents. Where do you begin?

Piloting

The first step, before you apply the survey in earnest, is to carry out a *pilot* exercise. On a few occasions, I've known managers to hesitate at this point. 'Look,' they say, 'why do we need to pilot it? We've spent weeks working on this questionnaire. Surely it's now as good as it's going to get.'

The answer is that the questionnaire is almost certainly *not* 'as good as it's going to get'. I've known very few questionnaires that haven't been substantially improved after piloting, and I've known a fair number where potentially serious problems have been spotted at this stage.

The problem is that, up to now, the questionnaire hasn't been seen by anyone (with the possible exception of the union representative) who's actually going to have to complete it. It's been scrutinized very carefully by you and possibly by the consultant working with you, but the two of you have been so heavily

105

involved in the whole process that you probably can't see the wood for the trees. It's been examined by the senior management team and by the line managers, but they probably won't have actually tried completing the form. Even the union or staff representatives will probably have examined the questionnaire from an employee relations perspective, rather than to improve its design.

As a result, all this screening is still far from infallible. It's quite possible, for instance, that none of the above would have spotted the use of a technical reference which might be meaningful to management (and even perhaps to the unions) but not to rank-and-file employees. Equally, none might have spotted a potential ambiguity.

It's *always* worth conducting a pilot exercise, no matter how confident you are about the quality of the survey. Nine times out of ten it will bring you some improvement, minor or major. On the tenth time, at least you'll have the reassurance of knowing that you're unlikely to have included any significant errors.

So how do you go about conducting the pilot survey? The first step is to select your pilot sample, usually a sub-sample of your intended survey group. If you were intending to conduct a survey in the Grommet Finishing Department, for instance, you might select a small number of them – four or five is usually sufficient – and pilot the questionnaire amongst these.

If you can avoid it, it's generally not a good idea to survey the same respondents twice. In other words, if a respondent has been asked to complete the pilot questionnaire, then he or she should not normally be asked to complete the final questionnaire as well. If nothing else, you'll probably find that some people will be irritated by having to complete the same questionnaire (more or less) twice. If their irritation becomes common knowledge that can easily undermine the credibility of the survey.

If you're looking at a fairly small population, then you may feel reluctant to 'waste' potential respondents by using them in the pilot exercise. Of course, if the questionnaire doesn't change (or changes only slightly) as a result of the pilot, then you might not have a problem – you could just include the pilot respondents in your final sample. But, if you can avoid it, it's better not to take the risk.

An alternative, which is often appropriate, is to pilot the questionnaire amongst a different, but similar, population. So, for example, if you're intending ultimately to survey the Grommet Finishing Department, it might be helpful to pilot the questionnaire in the Grommet Setting Department, which employs very similar categories of staff doing fairly similar work.

Once you've decided where you're going to pilot the questionnaire, you can then select your pilot respondents more or less at random. These respondents should then be asked to complete the questionnaire as if they were doing so as part of a 'real' survey.

Briefing the pilot group

We'll come in a moment to look at how you should present the survey to respondents and the workforce at large. Ideally, though, you should ensure that there is widespread awareness of the aims and nature of the survey among the whole workforce, with particular attention to the group that is to be surveyed, *even before you carry out the pilot exercise.* If there isn't widespread understanding of what you're up to, you'll probably find that misapprehensions grow up all too rapidly. Similarly, you should ensure that the pilot respondents fully understand their role. They are not themselves being surveyed, but are contributing to the design process.

Once the pilot group has completed the survey, you will probably learn a lot just from examining their responses. For example, if several of them have produced an unexpected response – as in the question about pensions quoted in the previous chapter – then that may indicate that the question is prone to misinterpretation or ambiguity. If several have failed to complete a particular question or section, this might mean that the question is not easily comprehensible or that the instructions are not clear. If there is an unexpectedly large number of erasures or crossings-out, this again might indicate confusion or a lack of clarity.

If you wish, you might improve the piloting process by asking respondents to jot down their opinions on the form as they go through it. If one of them finds a question unclear or ambiguous, then he or she can put a note to this effect next to it. If they don't understand the instructions or they're uncertain about what kind of answer is required, this too can be noted.

If you're preparing to conduct a survey across a very large

population or if the questionnaire format is particularly compli-
cated, it may also be worth trying to obtain more extensive views
from the pilot group. This can most effectively be achieved by
organizing a follow-up discussion which will allow you to discuss
in detail any areas where you have particular concerns. You may
also find that, once the group relaxes, members will begin to
express views which they felt reluctant to note on paper. For
instance, people are sometimes slow to admit that they found a
question complex or confusing, in case the comment is seen as a
reflection on their own abilities. However, in a group discussion,
once one person tentatively admits that he or she found the question slightly confusing, others will chip in, 'Yes, now you come
to mention it, I must say I wasn't entirely sure what that question
was getting at either . . . '

By the time you've completed the pilot, you should have identified most, if not all, of the potential problems that are likely to
arise with the questionnaire. This is not to say that the process is
fool-proof – there is always the possibility that some ambiguity or
potential source of confusion will still slip through the net. As we
suggested earlier, you can always bet that somebody, somewhere
will misinterpret something, however remote the possibility might
appear.

Presenting the questionnaire

Once you've completed the pilot, you can then redraft the questionnaire to take account of any insights you've received. And,
finally, you're ready to go with the full sample. Well, almost. As
we indicated above, before you begin to conduct the survey
proper, you need to ensure that everyone is fully aware of what
you're up to and what you're trying to achieve. We'll assume
that, as you've gone through the stages outlined in the preceding
chapters, you've been keeping both management and workforce
(not to mention the workforce's representatives, where that's relevant) informed of how you're progressing.

Yet even if you have been keeping people informed through
all the preliminary stages, it's usually worth making a special effort
immediately before you start conducting the formal survey. People
tend to be even more suspicious of written surveys than of other

kinds of employee research. If you're allowing the employees time to complete the question in working hours, then there is a danger that the whole process will resemble an examination – and nobody likes examinations. Moreover, people will be suspicious as to why you've chosen them – or why you haven't chosen them. Some respondents will assume that the questionnaire is somehow intended as a test of their personal abilities, and that they can 'pass' or 'fail'. Others will assume that the questionnaire is in some way designed to 'catch them out'.

So, before you begin to conduct the formal questionnaire – and ideally even before you begin to pilot it – go through the communication process again. If you are making use of any third-party consultants, explain who these are, why they've been involved and what their role is going to be. In many cases, the primary concern of employees – and one which will, quite rightly, be emphasized by any union groups involved – will be the issue of confidentiality. What reassurance do they have that their views won't get straight back to management?

Clearly, you can provide no absolute proof that confidentiality will be maintained. Nevertheless, if you make a point of demonstrating that the questionnaires will be anonymous, that the analysis will be carried out away from the organization and that, ideally, the survey will be administered by a third-party, then you should dispel most people's fears. And if you've also taken care to explain exactly who the third-party is, then that should increase confidence still further.

Resistance to the survey

In general terms, the more you can prepare the ground at this stage, the less likely you are to meet resistance. It is worth remembering that this kind of resistance can be active or passive. Active resistance can be more disruptive but is ultimately less damaging. There are numerous examples of surveys where either employees have refused to co-operate or where unions have instructed their members not to participate. Sometimes this has occurred in response to genuine provocation – perhaps where management have attempted to lie about their intentions or where they have tried to misuse the survey process in some way.

More commonly, though, this kind of resistance stems from a simple breakdown in communications. Management haven't taken the time to explain what they're up to, they've allowed speculation and rumour to run rife, or they've tried to bulldoze the whole process through without proper consultation. This kind of non-co-operation can be highly frustrating if you're on the receiving end. But, at the worst, it usually only means that you've wasted the time and money spent on preparing the survey, as well as souring your industrial relations still further; quite often, a little judicious behind-the-scenes work can get the show on the road again.

Passive resistance, on the other hand, can be potentially much more damaging. This is the situation where the employees nominally go along with the whole exercise, but refuse either to take it seriously or to answer honestly. You might, for example, find that respondents deliberately tick those responses that are likely to prove most disruptive to the organization. This is a much more insidious process. While the survey is being conducted, you assume that everything is going all right. Even when you come to analyse the results you don't realize that there's a problem, though you might be a little surprised by some of the findings. But when you've completed the survey, you may end up taking action which is not only unnecessary but also potentially damaging to the organization. This is the worst possible scenario – when the survey actually impairs your decision-making capability. It happens very rarely, which is some consolation, and it certainly won't happen if you follow the above advice. But it's always worth keeping in mind on those occasions when you're tempted (or impatient colleagues try to persuade you) to cut corners.

Conducting the survey

You're now at last ready to start conducting the formal survey. You should already have decided, in selecting your sample and designing the questionnaire, how you were going to do so. Let's take a few moments to have a look at the various options open to you, and at the pros and cons of each in an employment context. The following are likely to be the most relevant approaches:

Questionnaires completed through personal interviews – this is the process that most of us are familiar with through market-research surveys and opinion polls. We've all been stopped (or tried hard to avoid being stopped) by the person with the clipboard outside the shopping centre who asks you how many bars of soap you buy per year. In this case, the researcher simply spends time with you running through a series of predetermined questions, noting the answers down. The same process can, of course, be carried out by telephone.

This approach is particularly useful for market research and opinion polls because it allows the researcher to collect a large amount of data in a comparatively short time. It is also particularly helpful where you don't have easy access to the potential sample. However, these considerations are not particularly relevant in an employment context. You won't normally be in the position of having to produce findings overnight, so you can allow a reasonable time to collect and analyse the data. You also have complete access to the relevant sample, so there's nothing to be gained from hanging about outside the office door waiting to interview people! In short, you're unlikely to use the personal interview as a basis for completing the formal questionnaire – it's better to restrict the use of interviews to the exploratory and follow-up stages.

Questionnaires completed by respondents in their own time – the self-completed questionnaire is also widely used in market research. Probably the most common examples are those that often accompany the guarantees for electrical and other consumer goods, or the readership surveys that are often found in magazines. In these cases, the respondent has a free choice as to whether to complete the questionnaire and does so in his or her own time. Quite often, the researchers will offer some incentive to complete and return the form – perhaps a prize draw from completed responses.

The primary benefit of this approach is that, if you can afford the postage, it enables you to reach a potentially very large sample. If you mail to, say, 10,000 people, then even a 10% response will give you a sizeable sample. The approach also involves a comparatively low use of the researchers' time –

you don't have to spend days on end standing about outside Sainsbury's.

The primary drawback of this approach lies in the low response rate. Even if you do make significant efforts, by offering incentives and sending reminders, you'll still need to distribute at least five or six times more questionnaires than the minimum you need for your purposes. Moreover, it's much harder to structure the sample. You have no control over which recipients will choose to respond. Nevertheless, this approach can sometimes be useful in an employment context, particularly if you want to survey a very large sample. If you're a company of 25,000 employees and you want to conduct a survey across the whole organization, you may have no choice but to do it this way. Despite the drawbacks, this method does mean that you can survey very large numbers comparatively cheaply.

Questionnaires completed by the respondents in working time – this third approach is the most valuable in an employment context, so long as you can afford the necessary resources. Most commonly, the respondents are gathered in a room and asked to complete the questionnaire before returning to work. If the sample is large (or the only available room is small), then the process might be repeated several times.

Clearly, this approach has a number of advantages. You can ensure that the *whole* sample completes the questionnaire (unless, as occasionally happens, you get someone who directly refuses). This in turn means that you can structure the sample very carefully to ensure that it reflects the characteristics of the overall population.

Because the process is supervised, the researchers can also ensure that respondents fully understand the purpose, content and structure of the survey. If respondents are unclear about instructions or the meaning of a particular question, the researchers can provide clarification.

Finally, the survey can be completed comparatively quickly, with the information often gathered within a day or two. Although most employee surveys will not be time-critical in the sense that political opinion polls are, it is always helpful to save time. After all, the quicker you can obtain the information, the quicker you can start taking the action needed.

For these reasons, it is preferable to conduct employee surveys in this way, if at all possible. The primary disadvantage of this approach is simply that it requires a heavy investment of management (or consultant) time. You may have to supervise the completion of questionnaires over several days. And, of course, if you do want to survey a very large sample, it may simply be impractical.

Postal questionnaires

We'll assume that, depending on numbers and practical issues, you decide to use the second or third option above. For the second option – that is, sending the questionnaire to respondents to complete in their own time – the procedure is fairly straightforward. You simply distribute the questionnaires to respondents at either their work locations or their home addresses. If the survey covers any particularly contentious or personal issues, the use of the home address can sometimes be helpful in emphasizing the confidentiality of the exercise. It also helps indicate that the process is outside normal management relationships.

Take particular care to ensure that the design and instructions are clear. The respondents won't have any opportunity to ask questions. If they're confused about something, the chances are that they won't bother to ring up and ask. They'll just decide not to complete the questionnaire.

Remember to put a 'return by' date on the questionnaire. It's easy to forget – but if there isn't a deadline, people will put off completing the questionnaire because it isn't urgent. And then they'll never get round to doing it. My experience of carrying out research by mail suggests that there are usually two 'peaks' of response – the first is immediate and the second is just before (or sometimes just after) the closing date.

If you're able to do so, it's a good idea for the questionnaires to be returned to an address other than that of the employing organization. Once again, this reinforces the respondents' confidence in the confidentiality of the survey. If you're employing a third-party to conduct the survey, well and good. In that case, the questionnaires can simply be returned to the consultants' office address. Even if you're not, though, it's worth using a Post Office box number or some similar device. This may seem like overkill, but the more you can demonstrate that the survey is outside normal management structures and rules, the more likely you are to get honest responses.

Make every effort you can to encourage people to respond. It may even be appropriate to offer some form of incentive – a prize draw from the returned entries for a bottle of Champagne or the like. This is usually worthwhile, though you may feel that it introduces an inappropriate air of flippancy into the exercise. On the other hand, it can often serve as a valuable role in demonstrating that the exercise isn't a po-faced, intimidating scientific process. If you can manage to persuade people that the survey is fun (unlikely as that may sound), you'll get them to respond with much more alacrity.

One final point: if respondents are going to have to send the questionnaire back through the post, make sure you provide them with post-paid, *pre-addressed* envelopes. Recipients are much more likely to bother replying if they don't actually have to do very much. But, just because you have sent pre-addressed envelopes, don't forget also to put the address on the form. There are bound to be one or two people who lose the envelope but still want to reply.

On-site questionnaires

If you decide to provide working time for the questionnaires to be completed, the process is also straightforward. Again, though, it's a good idea to follow a few basic common-sense guidelines.

First of all, you need to provide a suitable room. Ideally, this should be somewhere separate from the respondents' normal working environment – as with the mailed questionnaire, it's useful to stress the distinction from standard organizational practices. Depending on the sample size, the room will probably need to be fairly large, with provision for the respondents to sit at tables while they complete the questionnaire. I have occasionally come across surveys where the organization has asked respondents to fill in a questionnaire balanced on their knees. This doesn't do a lot either for legibility or for clarity of thought.

The most appropriate room is usually somewhere like the staff canteen or a meeting room. If you don't have a large enough room available, you can always do it in shifts, though that will obviously take up more of your (or the consultant's) time. Some organizations simply make a room available, along with a stack of questionnaires, and ask respondents to turn up as they wish. This has the advantage of offering flexibility, but it does reduce your ability to ensure that the whole sample completes the questionnaire.

By and large, therefore, it's better to fix a time for the exercise. Don't forget to clear it with all the relevant line managers and supervisors – preferably in writing, so that no one can claim later that they didn't know. And ensure that the managers understand the practical implications: that their employees will be tied up for some considerable time, that they'll have to leave the workplace, that they shouldn't be interrupted in the middle, and so on. It's astonishing how managers can fail to take in this kind of information when it suits them, so do make sure that the message is clear.

Advise the respondents beforehand about what's going to happen, what time they should turn up, and where. You should have been keeping all the employees – and especially the selected sample – fully informed, so it should come as no surprise. Let them know how long the process is going to take. (It's no good holding the exercise at 2.30 in the afternoon, only to find that three or four people have got to disappear because they've got a dental appointment at 3.) If people have queries or problems about the exercise, encourage them to come and talk to you beforehand. And try to make the exercise sound as informal as possible, and mention that their managers and supervisors have agreed to release staff for the purpose.

Prepare the room by making sure that there are enough chairs and tables for all those involved. Make sure that there are writing implements – the best combination is probably pencils and erasers. When the respondents arrive in the room, encourage them to sit where they want to. Don't make the exercise too formal – it's a survey, not a school examination. There's nothing secret about the exercise, so if people want to chat, let them. But do encourage respondents not to talk about the survey until they've completed it. You want to hear their personal, individual views, not what they've been persuaded to say by old loud-mouthed Trevor in the corner.

Hand out the questionnaires and ask the respondents to complete them. Once in a while, you may get someone who, for whatever reason, claims not to be able to spare the time – can he or she take the form away and complete it at another time? Well, in the final analysis, there's not much you can do to prevent this. But try very hard to discourage it. Firstly, you'll probably find that, despite their earnest protestations, such individuals won't get round to filling in the form after all. Secondly, you don't want to encourage anyone else to follow their example. The best tack in this situation is to point out that you need the questionnaires completed straightaway. If the individual doesn't want to take part, that's fair enough, but in that case you'll have to exclude him or her from the survey. That generally does the trick.

Make sure that you've allowed sufficient time for people to complete the questionnaire to their satisfaction. Obviously people will complete it at different rates,but try to ensure that the slower ones don't feel intimidated or rushed. Let people know beforehand how much time they've got and encourage them to take as much of this as they want. After all, the slower ones may simply be providing you with more detail.

As the questionnaires are completed, you can collect them up, although an alternative and probably slightly preferable method is to have an equivalent of a ballot box – a large box with a slot into which people can post their questionnaires as they finish them. If the box is lockable, so much the better. If the exercise is being conducted by a consultant, the box is an additional indication of confidentiality and can remain locked until he or she is off-site. Even if you're not using a consultant, it is still a valuable indication that the completed surveys will not be accessible to unauthorized personnel.

Once the respondents have all finished and the box is full, the formal survey is finally complete. Thank the respondents and explain to them what's going to happen next. In particular, do let them know when they can expect to get some feedback on the results of the survey. If people have devoted time and effort to participating in a survey, it's only common courtesy to let them know something about the outcome – we'll come on to this process soon.

You're now ready to move on to the most difficult stage of all, trying to make some sense of the mass of information you've collected. And that's where we turn our attention next.

Summary

- Use a pilot survey to iron out problems
- Brief the pilot group – and the rest of the workforce – before you carry out the pilot exercise
- Keep a look out for active and passive resistance
- Assess the options of personal interviews, postal questionnaires and on-site questionnaires
- Preserve confidentiality at all times.

Chapter Eight

The Written Survey:
4 – What Do Your Findings Mean?

'Only connect'

E.M. Forster, Howards End

In a sense, all you've done so far is the easy bit. You've certainly got a lot of data, but anyone can collect data. We all do it all the time – watching television, listening to the radio, reading newspapers, talking to our friends and colleagues. The real trick is to take the plethora of information that we're given, make sense of it, and then use it to improve our decision-making capability. For example, if a colleague happens to mention over coffee that there are roadworks on the motorway, the comment might well go in one ear and out the other. On the other hand, you might relate it to a further bit of information – that your spouse has asked you to collect him or her from the station at 6.15. You put two and two together, and decide to try another route, with the result that you avoid the tailbacks and get there on time (unless you have my luck, in which case you get caught behind a slow-moving tractor for five miles).

When you're trying to make sense of data, you have to pay attention to several factors. First, you need to spot what data is likely to be significant; often that won't be obvious until you've combed through all the information. Second, you need to spot the connections between the various pieces of data. You need to make a mental link between the facts that there are roadworks on the motorway and that you need to pick up your spouse. In many cases, the links will be much less obvious – if a friend was coming to visit you that evening, it might not occur to you to

118

think where he or she was coming from or which route they'd use. Third, you need to spot the pieces of information you don't have but which might be inferred from the data in front of you. Suppose two colleagues separately mention to you that they were late for work that morning because of the traffic. You may not realize that both of them had got caught in the same roadworks that morning, although you *could* have inferred it if you'd known which route your colleagues normally took into work.

The mental processes involved in analysing survey-data are just the same as these day-to-day exercises. The only difference is that you need to be rather more systematic in going through the three stages above. Before we move on, let's just recap:

- try to spot the significant pieces of information – and remember that their significance may become evident only in the context of the overall findings
- try to spot the significant links between pieces of data – and again these may only be apparent once you've been through all the information
- try to spot the pieces of information that you haven't got, but which you might reasonably infer from the data in front of you. Don't worry if some of your inferences are slightly speculative at this stage – you'll get the chance to check them out later.

Analysing the statistics

In a moment, we'll move on to look at how you can apply these processes to the survey findings. Before we do that, let's linger briefly on the question of how you carry out the numerical analysis of the questionnaires. The best advice is: don't bother – get someone else to do it for you. Unless you're dealing with a *very* small sample (say, 30 or less), you'll find that the process of adding up the responses and then analysing the results extremely time-consuming – not to say frustrating.

If you do decide bravely to tackle it yourself, don't try to do it by hand. It's much easier, in these days of high technology, to use a computer. If you have access to one, you can use one of the specialist research databases, which can do all kinds of wonderful statistical tricks. If you don't have access to one of these and you're carrying out a fairly simple survey, you can probably carry out adequate numerical analysis using a standard database or even a spreadsheet package.

But, quite frankly, while this may be an entertaining experience for masochists, it's not usually worth the trouble. There are plenty of specialist software bureaux which will carry out this kind of numerical analysis for a comparatively modest sum. Against the overall investment you'll be making in the survey, the cost is likely to be fairly negligible – and certainly justified for the sake of retaining your sanity. In addition, at little extra cost such bureaux are usually able to produce further statistical analysis, where appropriate (calculating means, standard deviations, measures of statistical significance and correlations between different findings). Few of these are likely to be critical for the purposes of an employee survey, but they can be interesting – and occasionally they can be useful as additional evidence in support of a particular hypothesis.

If you *are* going to use a bureau, however, make sure you involve them from the earliest stages of designing the questionnaire. You'll often find that they have invaluable suggestions to improve it, especially to make it easier to analyse. And even if they don't, they'll want to 'pre-code' the questionnaire to make their own data input easier. 'Pre-coding' is the inclusion of a scoring mechanism, usually down one side of each page. The questionnaire responses can then be turned into coded form, so that a keyboard operator can input the data directly, without having to scan through each question individually. If you don't involve the bureau at the design stage, and therefore don't pre-code the questionnaire, you'll find that the cost of the numerical analysis will be correspondingly higher.

Breaking down the results

Generally speaking, the bureau will provide you with page after page of numerical analysis in the form of computer printout. You will receive the level of data you ask for, so take care to specify every kind of analysis that you're likely to need. At the very least, this will include totalled responses for each question. But, where appropriate, you should also obtain sub-totals for any relevant groups within the overall sample. The best approach is to go back to your sample design. Look again at the range of variables that you identified as significant. In general, you'll want to obtain sub-totals against each of these variables, so that you can assess whether there are significant trends evident between the various groups.

These sub-analyses will help you decide whether there are any needs, issues or problems which are relevant to particular groups – for example, whether the women in the sample have different needs from the men or whether junior staff have different concerns from more senior staff. You can then target your activities and decision-making accordingly.

When the wad of computer print-outs – usually page after page after page of them – land with a thud on your desk, your first reaction will probably be something approaching despair. How on earth are you going to make sense of this mass of closely (and often badly) printed data? What do all these numbers *mean*? So let's press on, and look at this more closely.

Handling the data

The first, straightforward piece of advice is: don't be intimidated. Computer printout is probably one of the least user-friendly media in the world, but the information it contains will actually be fairly simple. When you first go through the printout, it's a good idea to be armed with a few highlighter pens of various colours, so that you can mark the bits of information that are likely to be relevant. You'll probably also want to scribble notes in the margins, as you come across elements that appear to be interesting or significant. Don't worry too much at this stage about what you can (or can't) prove – just note anything that strikes your attention. You'll have plenty of opportunity for discarding data later on, but you don't want to miss anything that might potentially be worth thinking about.

Before you run in detail through the various totals, return to the original theories you were trying to explore in the survey. Keep them in mind as you examine the results. For example, we had a number of theories about the possible causes of the problems we'd identified in the Grommet Finishing Department. We then produced a questionnaire designed to obtain detailed information on the respondents' opinions about these issues.

We now need to go through the results of the survey to see whether the responses appear to support any or all of our theories. Above all, you're looking for results which appear striking or unexpected. As we've repeatedly stressed in the previous chapters, it's probably not worth devoting too much attention to 'borderline' results, since you'll very probably have difficulty persuading anyone to act on them anyway. For example, if 25% of the respondents express dissatisfaction with supervisory style in the department, then that's probably not worth worrying about too much. On the other hand, if 75% of the department express dissatisfaction, then it looks as if you've got a problem and you need to decide what to do about it.

But, you might ask, what happens if, say, 55% of the workforce express dissatisfaction with the supervisory style? Does that mean you have a problem? Do you need to do anything about it? There's no simple answer to this. If you were conducting academic research or a political opinion poll, then you would probably conduct a test of statistical significance to assess the likelihood that this result accurately reflected the opinions of the overall population. In an employment context, it's probably not worth the effort. Provided you're confident that the result is accurate to within, say, 10 percentage points, it doesn't much matter to you whether the 'true' figure should be 45% or 65%. The important question, as far as you're concerned, is not how accurate this figure is (within reason). The important question is: in practical terms, what does this figure actually *mean*? Does it mean that there's significant dissatisfaction? Does it mean that there's an urgent problem? What should you do about it?

The trouble is, of course, that it's very difficult to give an absolute meaning to these kinds of findings. Is 55% a high level of dissatisfaction? Is it an average level? Or is it (despite appearances) actually a fairly low level? If every other department in the organization or every other organization in the country has a dissatisfaction level of 85%, then this particular department is actually doing rather well. In other words, many of these findings only really have any meaning in relative terms – you can only interpret them by comparison with other departments, other organizations or other times.

This is a real difficulty. When organizations are first contemplating conducting an employee survey, it's often worth warning them not to be too depressed by the initial results. I've quite often come across surveys which have revealed dissatisfaction levels of 60% or more in virtually every area examined. 'But this is disastrous!' the managers say. 'We knew we had a bit of a problem, but we never expected anything like this! We've got to take dramatic action straightaway!'

Yet, in relative terms, these results are probably not as bad as they appear. It's important to remember that the overall level of results in a given survey can easily be distorted by a variety of factors. If this is the first opportunity that respondents have had to express their views, it's hardly surprising that they'll take their chance to express every possible dissatisfaction. And, when it comes down to it, very few of us can claim to be thoroughly satisfied with every aspect of our employment. So these apparently high levels of dissatisfaction might in fact reflect little more than a general desire from respondents to make their voices heard. If there are other channels – consultative committees, liaison meetings, etc. – through which respondents can express (and get resolved) minor dissatisfactions, then you'll probably obtain fewer expressions of dissatisfaction through the survey.

So how do you get behind these general distorting factors to find out what the results really mean? There *are* some ways you can do this, as we discussed earlier. The most effective is to repeat the survey at regular interviews. This has two advantages: firstly, people get used to surveys, so they don't see them as the only opportunity to make their views known; secondly, the sequence provides a context within which you can evaluate the individual results. In other words, you concentrate less on the absolute results from any individual year and more on the trends and variations from year to year. If the level of dissatisfaction in one area decreases from, say, 55% to 40%, whereas in another area it increases from 55% to 70%, then you can concentrate your efforts in the second area.

Most organizations, though, unless they have a high level of resources available, won't want to conduct regular surveys of this kind. An alternative approach is to conduct the survey across several divisions of the organization apart from the area you want to investigate. The findings from this other part (or parts) act like the 'control' sample in a scientific experiment – in other words, it provides a context in which to evaluate responses from the area you're interested in. For example, if 60% of respondents elsewhere are dissatisfied with the working accommodation, whereas there's a 75% level of dissatisfaction in the department under investigation, then you can concentrate your energies in this area.

You should also examine trends and variations between the various sub-groups – the significant variables that you identified in drawing up your original sample. Again, the absolute level of responses is likely to be less important than the relative levels. For example, if there is a difference in responses between senior grades and junior grades, you will need to target your resultant action accordingly. Similarly, you might find that there appear to be differences between, say, men and women or individuals in different job categories.

It's a good idea, when you're first going through the results, simply to highlight any obvious divergences from the norm, even if you've no idea what their significance might be. If, for instance, men and women have tended to give broadly similar responses except to one specific question, then highlight that question, even if you can't for the moment think of any reason why there should be any variation in that particular case. You can then sit back and think about it, and, if you feel it's worthwhile, explore the issue in more detail in the follow-up research (which we'll come on to in the next chapter). You might ultimately decide that the variation is no more than a 'blip' – simply the result of sampling error or a fluke response. On the other hand – and this happens quite often – you may stumble across some contributory factor which wouldn't otherwise have occurred to you. To take a simple example, you might find that significantly more women than men have expressed dissatisfaction with the office accommodation. At first, you can't think of any good reason why this should be, but you highlight it anyway. When you go back to look at the departments under review, you realize that, by coincidence, the majority of the women are in one part of the accommodation while the majority of the men are elsewhere. So, as it turns out, the significant difference is not gender, but *where the respondents happen to be sited.*

Spotting the links

This last example brings us on to the next stage of interpretation. You've now been through the print-outs and highlighted all the extreme results, all the apparent deviations from the norm – in short, all the apparently significant pieces of data. Your next step is to start thinking about what these pieces of information might mean and, in particular, to start trying to identify any apparent linkages or connections.

In some cases, these links will probably be fairly obvious. For example, you might find, in particular departments or among particular job categories, high levels of dissatisfaction with both working practices and working conditions. A little thought will probably indicate to you that the people concerned are undertaking comparatively unpleasant work, and that the two findings are really just reflecting different aspects of this unpleasantness.

Other links will be less obvious, but perhaps potentially more revealing. For example, you might find that a much larger proportion of women in a particular department express dissatisfaction both with working practices and with management style. A superficial response might be to assume that this is just a fluke result, but more thoughtful investigation, perhaps conducted during the follow-up research, could lead you to a different conclusion. You might discover, for example, that a sexist supervisor tends to give the female members of the department, regardless of grade, the more mundane and mindless work; the more interesting and challenging work is usually given to the men. In other words, two results which could have quite separate causes in fact reflect the same phenomenon. In this case, the link has actually highlighted a specific problem which, provided you're prepared to grasp the nettle, you can probably resolve fairly easily.

Don't jump to conclusions!

At the same time, in identifying these links, you need always to be vigilant to avoid jumping to the wrong conclusions. When we discussed the issues involved in sample design, we referred to the need to be aware of any close correlations between *apparently* separate variables such as age and grade. This becomes particularly critical when you are analysing these variables as sub-groups in your overall findings.

You might find, for instance, that the older staff tend to express much higher levels of satisfaction with supervisory style. Fine, you think. People grow older, get more mellow and mature, are more tolerant. Some of them are getting close to retirement – they can afford not to worry too much about how they're treated. It all makes sense.

Except, of course, that you also notice that more senior staff tend to express higher levels of satisfaction with supervisory style. Well, that's not surprising, you think. People take on more senior jobs, they get some supervisory responsibilities of their own, they understand the pressures that supervisors are under – obviously they'll get more tolerant of the way supervisors behave.

And yet, of course, there's a close correlation between these two groups – the group of older staff may in large part be *the same* as the group of more senior staff. So, in effect, you now have two different explanations for the same phenomenon. Which is correct? Do people tend to be more satisfied with the supervisory style because they're older and more mature? Or only when they start to take on some supervisory responsibilities of their own? Or, perhaps most likely, is it a combination of the two?

In this case, it probably doesn't matter too much, although it might be rather disturbing if the only people who were satisfied with the supervisory style were the supervisors themselves! In other cases, though, this confusion could seriously distort your resultant management decisions. I've seen quite a number of surveys where women have characteristically expressed considerably higher levels of dissatisfaction than men. If you happen to be presenting the results to a smug (and often all-male) Board or management team, it will simply confirm all their prejudices. 'Just what I've always suspected,' they say. 'I always knew that women were more unstable than men. Look at this lot. Always whingeing on about something. There's no wonder that they all go off after two years to get married and have kids . . . '

This incisive analysis fails to take account of the fact that those expressing high levels of dissatisfaction are not only women – they may well also tend to be low-graded. And you're quite likely to find, if you come to investigate the issue in more detail, that their dissatisfaction stems much more from their comparatively lowly position in the organization than from the fact that they happen to be of a particular sex.

As this example indicates, if you don't think very carefully about the causes and effects involved, you may simply end up using the data to pander to your own prejudices. If you have strong preconceptions, it's all too easy to seize upon a particular result as evidence, without thinking through the host of other contributory factors involved. If a manager has got it into his head that a particular department are a bunch of whingers, then high levels of dissatisfaction will simply confirm this. Unless you push quite hard, you might find it difficult to suggest that there could actually be a *cause* for their dissatisfaction.

The simple message arising from this is: keep an open mind. Don't jump to conclusions. Weigh up all the issues. Think about the possible links between the various sub-groups. Don't let your prejudices overrule your better judgement. And if you're in any doubt about the implications of a particular piece of information, don't make assumptions. Highlight it – and then put it aside until you're able to investigate it in more detail.

'Hidden' data

This brings us to the third stage of the interpretative process – trying to identify the pieces of information you don't have but which you might be able to deduce or infer from the information you *have* collected. This process is a little like those old childhood puzzles where you have to make sense of an apparently baffling story by supplying one additional extra detail. It is often crucial to be able to go beyond the obvious factors to identify some further issue – which may actually be at the root of the problems you're investigating. Indeed, it's probably not an exaggeration to say that it is this which often distinguishes the most successful surveys.

There is no simple trick to spotting 'hidden' information in survey findings. The process is a little like an astrophysicist inferring the existence of a black hole. You observe the behaviour of the surrounding phenomena and try to ascertain whether there is anything surprising – any factors not explained by the available data. Alternatively, you might look for the existence of apparent similarities between different sub-groups which might point to the existence of some wider cause. For example, if staff across three different departments express similar dissatisfactions with their supervisors, you might ask whether there is some linking factor. This might be, for example, that all three departments are engaged in similar kinds of operations, and that these operations, by their very nature, compel the supervisors to behave unsatisfactorily. Or you might find that all three departments report ultimately to one manager – and that this manager is actually the root-cause of the supervisors' behaviour.

You might also encounter some apparently baffling responses. Suppose, for instance, that your survey covers issues such as career development and promotion. Three or four years ago, the organization revamped all its career-planning mechanisms. You introduced specialist career planners, a computerized career-management system, and a highly sophisticated developmental appraisal system. You've conducted previous surveys on these issues over the past couple of years, and you've fine-tuned the new systems to take full account of employee opinion. On the whole, you're now pretty happy with the mechanisms and you believe that most of the employees are fairly satisfied too.

Nonetheless, you decide to conduct one further survey to check. When you get the results back, you find that, by and large, your views have been confirmed. However, the results are strangely polarized. In other words, although only a small proportion of the employees – some 20% or less – express significant dissatisfaction, those who are dissatisfied express *very* high levels of dissatisfaction. They like almost no aspect of the system, and they indicate that they are 'very unhappy' with most elements of the career-planning mechanism.

What is the explanation for this? It's probably difficult to say without some further investigation. Nevertheless, you might begin to draw up some hypotheses, drawing on the information available from the survey, as well as on your general knowledge of the organization. It might be, for instance, that although the system is generally good at selecting the right person for the job, the organization is ineffective at providing feedback to those not selected. In this case, the negative responses may come from those who saw themselves as contenders for a particular job and who felt slighted at not being selected. You clearly need to improve the provision of feedback. Alternatively, your hypothesis might be that, although in general the systems are effective, the organization has not been good at providing career-development opportunities for a particular group. For example, if the organization is largely comprised of professional staff, the support staff may feel that they are getting a raw deal.

In this kind of situation, it's all too easy to miss the full significance of the information you've gathered. You may feel so overjoyed that 60% of people are very happy with your mechanisms that you don't think to look closely at the 20% who aren't. Even if you do, you won't have any direct information on *why* they're discontented because you hadn't thought to ask the right questions. It's very important that you don't just jump at the obvious data, but also ask yourself if there are any less obvious factors, puzzling results or responses which might indicate concerns not directly covered in the survey.

Summary

- Spot the significant pieces of data and the links between them; use them to infer new information
- Employ specialist software bureaux for the numerical analysis
- Note down all obvious divergences from the norm
- Don't jump to conclusions!
- Remember the links between different variables
- Pick up the hints, explore the grey areas – the hidden information is often the most important

Chapter Nine

Following up the Survey

'The truth is rarely pure, and never simple'

Oscar Wilde, The Importance of Being Earnest

As we've indicated more than once in the preceding chapters, the formal, written questionnaire is only one element in the overall process. And yet it's all too common for managers to assume, once the written survey's out of the way, that their research is complete. 'That's it,' they say. 'We've found out what we needed to. Now we're ready to do something about it.'

Occasionally, this may be true. Once in a while, the written survey will reveal such a major, urgent, glaring problem that there's no time for further research. You've just got to take immediate action to put things right. If 99% of your employees indicate that they're on the point of going on strike about your bonus scheme, then probably it's a good idea to take some immediate action before they do just that. On the other hand, if the problem really is that serious, one would hope that you wouldn't need a survey to tell you about it!

In general, however, even the most urgent problem is best tackled through a further process of consultation and research, so long as it's clear that the research is leading somewhere and is not just an excuse for procrastination. If they're convinced you're going to take action, even the most militant union will usually stay away from the barricades long enough for you to consult with them and their members.

In short, the written survey should hardly ever be the end of the road. This is not to understate its value. It provides you with quantitative information. It allows you to confirm (or, just as important, to disprove) your initial theories. It highlights broad trends of opinion or attitudes which can inform your future decision-making. But, at the same time, a written questionnaire is a fairly blunt instrument. It tends (often deliberately) to exclude subtleties and shades of opinion. It encourages you to categorize responses rather than to investigate them. It usually closes down discussion rather than opening it up. In other words, the written questionnaire is a valuable but limited tool. And you should no more use it as the sole tool for organizational development than you'd use a hammer as the sole tool for mending your television set!

Summarizing the findings

The first step, which you should *always* take regardless of what you're intending to do next, is to produce a short and accessible summary of the survey findings. It's surprising how often managers fail to do this – or, at least, how often they produce a summary for their own bosses or colleagues, but not for the employees who've actually contributed to the survey. You should produce a summary which can be read quickly and easily both by the management team (including the Chief Executive, the Board and anyone else who's likely to have an interest) and by the rest of the workforce.

In practice, these may be two separate documents, in both style and content. The management summary, for instance, might be more formal, perhaps in the standard format of management reports. It might also highlight potential problems or areas of concern which you wouldn't necessarily want to highlight to the whole workforce. If the summary indicates a possible tendency towards demotivation, you might feel that it would be counterproductive to publish this to all the employees. In this case, you might feel, it is probably better to try to tackle the problem without making it explicit.

By contrast, the employee summary – unconstrained by the formal demands of management protocol – might well be a less formal, more accessible document. In particular, you can often make valuable use of graphics to illustrate the statistical findings of the survey in a clear and striking manner. This might involve standard graphs, histograms, pie-charts, etc., or it might involve some more imaginative graphics. I once saw the results of a survey in a record-manufacturing company presented as record-shaped pie-charts. I've also seen graphics selected to reflect the subject matter of the particular question – so that, for example, the various response-levels to a question about pay might be presented as pound-signs of different heights. If you can afford it – and if the summary is going out to a reasonably large group of employees – it's often worth employing a professional graphic designer to give shape to your design ideas. If you can't afford this or you don't think it's justified by the number of recipients, it's also worth remembering that many database packages now include a facility for translating tables of statistics directly into graphs. In these days of computerization, there's not usually much excuse for boring and unclear presentation.

It's also worth stressing that, although the management and employee summaries may differ slightly in presentation and content, they shouldn't usually differ significantly. For instance, while slight variations in emphasis may be permissible (as in the example quoted above), it's not a good idea to exclude significant data from one or other document. In particular, you shouldn't exclude major trends or findings from the employee summary just because they indicate negative responses. The primary objective of an employee survey, beyond simply obtaining information, is to promote trust, openness and communication. If the employees discover that managers are withholding information just because they're not happy with the findings, then you'll undermine much of the value of the exercise. If you can manage to produce just one document, for management and workforce alike, then so much the better.

Value of the summary

So why produce this summary, and what should you do with it? The summary will produce a number of benefits, some more obvious than others. Let's just run through some of the key ones:

- it enables you to clarify your own thoughts. It's usually a good idea to restrict the summary to no more than a couple of

A4 sides. The process of summarizing the survey's key findings is an invaluable discipline. It helps you decide which findings are the most important, which of your initial theories have been proved or disproved, and where you still need more information

• it's simply courteous to provide feedback to those who've taken part in the exercise. It's still not unknown for organizations to conduct employee surveys and then fail to inform respondents of the outcome. This is both rude and counterproductive: if you don't even bother to give them any feedback, respondents will think, what chance is there that you're actually going to take any action?

• it helps promote the unspoken agenda behind any employee survey – that of improving trust, communication and understanding within the organization. If the workforce accepts that management is prepared to provide honest feedback on their views, this is likely to promote a climate of trust. This in turn will make it easier for management to implement the actions that may be required in response to the survey

• finally, and perhaps most importantly, it provides a clear, precise basis for further discussion, investigation and action.

To achieve the above objectives, you need to produce the summary quickly – usually within a month of the survey's completion at the latest, unless it's a *very* complex document – and you need to distribute it to all those who are likely to have an interest. In many cases, this will mean not only the management team and the respondents but also the rest of the workforce. In more specialized cases, it may mean only particular divisions or departments. Make sure you include *all* relevant people – and, in particular, all those who are likely to be affected by any subsequent management actions or decisions. If the survey leads you to take action with a knock-on effect in other divisions, then it's a good idea to ensure that everyone involved understands the background.

Follow-up research

Once the summaries have been issued and everyone's had a chance to digest and think about the contents, then it's time to embark on follow-up research. This, as you'll recall from the 'hourglass' model, is the point where discussion opens out again. In other words, it's the point where you try to get behind the quantitative data you've gained through the written survey.

So how do you go about doing this? In broad terms, you need to revert to the investigatory techniques you employed during the first, exploratory stage of your research. As in that first stage, your aim is to encourage open, participative discussion. You're no longer trying to quantify or categorize data – you're trying to explore the subtleties, nuances and grey areas involved in people's responses.

In part, you can do this again through one-to-one interviews. You select a number of respondents, either from your original sample or from elsewhere in the group. This choice depends on whether your primary aim is to explore respondents' views further or to test out such views by appealing to others in the group. For instance, if the survey has led you to suspect that a large proportion of respondents are directly dissatisfied with the management style of their particular supervisor, you may feel that it is useful to test this theory by interviewing other members of the same work-group. Alternatively, you might feel that it would be more revealing to talk to some of your original respondents to explore in more detail the reasons for their dissatisfaction. It's worth remembering, in making this decision, that your aim at this stage is not to produce more quantifiable or statistically measurable data; it's to gain a fuller and clearer understanding of the data you've already got.

For this reason, you don't normally need to worry too much about the size and structure of your interview sample at this stage. Having said that, it's usually worth making some effort to ensure that your interviewees cover a cross-section of the major variables you identified in drawing up your original sample. After all, you want to cover as broad a range of respondents as possible.

Because the responses to the written survey were anonymous, you won't of course be able specifically to interview those respondents who expressed interesting views or concerns. This is a pity, because you will often be particularly keen to investigate further those responses which fall outside the mainstream or which indicate an extreme reaction. For instance, if you found a comment which read, say, 'DON'T TALK TO ME ABOUT SUPERVIS-

ORY STYLE. THE ONLY THING THAT STOPS ME RESIGNING IS THE THOUGHT OF MY PENSION . . . ', you might well be keen to find out what had inspired this vitriolic response.

One approach, rather than selecting your interviewees, is to ask explicitly for volunteers. You might, for example, write round to all the original respondents, saying something like:

> We would now like to conduct follow-up interviews with a number of those who completed the written questionnaire. We are particularly interested in hearing more detailed views about Section 5 ('Supervisory Style'), Section 7 ('Work Accommo- dation') and Section 10 ('Company Values'). If you would like to take part in these interviews, contact . . .

Of course, not all of those who expressed trenchant views in the questionnaire will be willing to do the same in public. But it's a fair bet that at least some of those who feel strongly about a given subject will be willing to do so. If you do adopt this tactic, remember that the resulting sample will not be representative. In this case, the respondents will have been consciously self-selected; along with a few loud-mouths, they should represent some inter- estingly extreme or unusual views. Your aim in interviewing them is to explore some of the more idiosyncratic – and therefore potentially problematic – views, not to obtain a general under- standing of the overall population.

I've occasionally known researchers come out of conducting interviews with two or three outspoken individuals and then report back, 'Well, that department's clearly entirely fed up with its management. If you don't take immediate action, you'll have a mutiny on your hands . . . ' It's not always easy to retain a sense of perspective when you're being harangued by the departmental malcontent, but you must do so – if you don't, you'll end up taking extreme and inappropriate action. On the other hand, don't just dismiss the malcontent's views, particularly if they appear to receive some support from the group generally. It's quite possible that he or she is merely giving more extreme expression to views that are more or less shared by everyone.

Once you've obtained your interviewees, you can then begin to conduct the interviews. As with the other elements of the survey, it's helpful to involve a third-party interviewer. It's much easier if the interviewee can feel reasonably confident that his or her views won't be fed directly back to management. For the same reason, it's once again a good idea to hold the interviews away from the normal workplace.

Conducting follow-up interviews

The aim of the interview is to encourage open discussion. You're not trying to carry out a face-to-face rerun of the written questionnaire, so don't simply go through a question-and-answer session based on the original form. The most profitable approach is usually to draw on the survey findings and to ask broad, open questions. In particular, it's often useful to explore the interviewee's reaction in those areas where the results have been surprising or unexpected to management. You might ask, for example:

> Did you notice that 75% of respondents expressed considerable dissatisfaction with the bonus scheme? Did that result surprise you?

Or, even more simply:

> 77% of respondents said that they were unhappy with the supervisory style of their department. What did you make of that result?

Most of us are flattered to be asked our opinion in this kind of situation, and you'll generally find that interviewees, once they relax, will be only too willing to give you the benefit of their views: 'I'm not surprised people don't like the bonus scheme. I mean, it pays well enough, but nobody really thinks it's fair. We see those lazy so-and-so's in packaging reaching their targets without breaking sweat, whereas we . . . ' or 'Well, I don't really think that's a fair response. Old Norman's a bit of a hard taskmaster and he certainly doesn't suffer fools gladly, but in my opinion that's the kind of supervisor you need to get things done . . . '

You'll often find that, whether the interviewee agrees or disagrees with the response, he or she will nonetheless give you an insight into why people have responded that way. In most cases, the interviewee will either want to explain why he or she (along with most of the rest of the group) holds a particular view, or why his or her views happen to disagree with everyone else's. Either way, it should help you to gain a clearer understanding both of the majority opinion and of any significant dissenting voices.

In the same way, you can use the interviews to explore some of the apparently interesting minority responses. For example, to go back to the survey on career development that we looked at in the last chapter, you might ask:

On the whole, it seemed as if most people were fairly happy with our approach to career development, as you saw. But there was a minority of respondents who seemed pretty unhappy with it – why do you think that might be?

If the interviewee happens to be part of the unhappy minority, he or she will probably tell you promptly enough. Yet even if the interviewee is personally happy with the system, he or she may well have a good idea of why others aren't. Once again, the interview should help you put some meaningful flesh on the bare bones of your statistical findings.

In conducting the interviews, do try to keep the discussion as open and participative as possible. In particular, try to avoid leading questions. Don't, for example, say:

You probably noticed that 75% of respondents claimed to be unhappy with the office accommodation. Quite frankly, that astonished us. After all, we've just finished spending £300,000 doing the place up. What's your feeling about that result?

You've certainly revealed where you – the management generally – stand on that issue. It'll take a brave interviewee to turn round after that and say, 'Well, I think it's fair enough. After all, the air conditioning still doesn't work properly. It's freezing in winter and boiling in summer. You can't open a window, and as for the decor . . . ' Most interviewees will just tell you what they've decided you want to hear. At best, you might get, 'Don't get me wrong. Personally, I'm happy enough, but I have heard one or two people complaining about the temperature . . . ' That tells you a bit, but you'd probably have got a lot more if you hadn't led the interviewee to start with.

It's generally best to conduct these interviews too on a 'semi-structured' basis. In other words, you should draw up a standard structure, identifying the range of issues that you want to investigate further. In most cases, these will arise naturally from the most significant findings of the formal survey. Alternatively, you may be seeking to confirm unexpected findings or you may want to explore some new ideas or theories that have arisen. Or you may be simply looking for more detailed information about the major trends of the survey.

This structure should assist you in retaining control of the interview. Although these interviews, like the preliminary ones, should aim to be open and participative, control is usually more important at this stage. In the initial, pre-questionnaire interviews, you were generally happy with the interview to develop in any direction, so long as it was providing you with useful information. It didn't much matter if interviewees strayed away from your questions on to their own hobby-horses, provided that these were relevant to your overall aims. After all, at that stage, a digression by the interviewee might well lead you to consider some new issue or aspect of the subject. And that, in turn, could lead you to draw up a more useful and accurate survey questionnaire.

In this follow-up stage, though, your aims are more focussed. You've identified the topics you want to explore and you've gathered a mass of data on these. Your objective now is to obtain a range of more detailed and subjective commentary on these issues, to allow you to go beyond the limitations of a formal questionnaire.

While you certainly want interviewees to talk as openly, broadly and frankly as possible about these topics, you don't really want the conversation to spread into new, unconsidered issues. It's not really much use to you if the interviewee suddenly says, 'Well, if you ask me, the *real* problem in this department is the way we recruit people . . . ', if that isn't an issue you've raised in the questionnaire. You might note it in the back of your mind for a future survey, but that's about as much as you can do.

This doesn't mean that, if a really critical new topic should emerge in the course of the interview, you should ignore it. Occasionally, despite your best efforts in the earlier stages, a totally unexpected but clearly important topic *will* arise at this stage. If that happens, you'll have no choice but to go back and collect further information, even if it means conducting an additional written survey. In general, though, if you've done your earlier work properly, it shouldn't happen. Otherwise, you should do your best to ensure that the interview maintains its focus on the issues you've highlighted. If the conversation does begin to drift into other areas, it's as well to say, as soon as you politely can, 'Clearly that's an interesting topic, but it's a whole new area. I'd like if we can to go back to the bonus scheme (or whatever) for a moment . . .'

Looking forward

Perhaps the most important benefit of the follow-up interview is that, in addition to providing more detailed information, it also allows you to look to the future. It enables you to gather views, not only on what's wrong with the organization, but also on what can be done to put this right. Of course, the written survey allows you to gather some information of this type. For instance, the questionnaire might well ask:

Which medium do you think management should use to achieve more effective communication? [tick one]

staff magazine/newspaper	[ ]
videos	[ ]
notice boards	[ ]
memoranda	[ ]
briefing groups	[ ]
trade unions	[ ]
etc.	

Implicitly, this question is asking the respondent to give a view on what management should do to improve its communications practices. On the whole, although it is certainly possible to ask forward-looking questions in a written questionnaire, the multiple-choice format tends primarily to encourage questions about the current state of affairs. In a restrictive format, it's much easier to ask a respondent what he or she thinks about the here-and-now than to seek views about how this should be changed.

This not only limits the kinds of data that are gathered by the survey, it also – if you're not careful – tends to endow the whole exercise with a rather negative tone. In other words, respondents spend all their time telling you what's wrong with the current state of affairs, and very little providing constructive opinions about what can be done to improve matters. Of course, this process can be cathartic. But I've sometimes known the simple act of conducting the survey to have a detrimental effect on morale among respondents: 'You know, until you asked me these questions I hadn't realized that things were so bad . . . ' Yet this may be only because you've focussed their attention on the problem areas and, even more importantly, you haven't given respondents the opportunity to provide positive views about how improvements can be made.

The follow-up interview lets you explore some of these more positive issues in a non-intimidatory way. You can usually do it through a sequence of questions along these lines:

> I notice that 69% of respondents expressed dissatisfaction about the amount of paperwork and petty bureaucracy they get involved in. What's your experience of that? Do you think it really is a problem?

Once the interviewee has given you the benefit of his or her opinions on the subject, you can then ask:

> Do you have any thoughts about how matters could be improved?

or

> So what would *you* like to see happen to improve things?

If you ask this kind of question in a formal, written questionnaire, the respondent will often feel that he or she has to come up with a well-thought-out, foolproof response, rather than an off-the-cuff answer that doesn't take account of all the issues. Respondents often end up thinking, 'Well, I've always thought we could improve things by doing away with the formal logging procedures, but management must have thought of that. There are probably dozens of good reasons why we can't do that, and I ought to be aware of them. So I can't put that down – they'll think I'm a total idiot . . . ' As a result, the intimidated employee just leaves the space blank.

In a relaxed, informal, conversational interview, it's obvious that you're not asking for anything foolproof. You're just seeking an off-the-top-of-the-head opinion, tapping into that vein of 'Well, I can't understand why management don't just . . . ' rumination that's the stuff of employee conversations over coffee or in the pub. Because, as we all know, in many cases managers *won't* have thought of the solutions that seem so obvious to the person doing the job. That's why employee suggestion schemes can be so valuable – and this way you don't even have to reward the suggestion if you don't want to!

Group workshops

Of course, one-to-one interviews are not the only medium for follow-up research. This kind of qualitative information can often be gathered even more effectively through the use of group discussions or workshops. The group approach has the disadvantage that it doesn't allow you to talk in depth with any single interviewee. On the other hand, it does have a number of significant advantages which it is worth recapping briefly.

The first, and most straightforward, of these is that it quite simply allows you to involve many more people. It's also usually easier to achieve a relaxed, participative atmosphere in a group discussion. There's always a danger, of course, that a single outspoken individual will dominate the group and distort its responses. For example, if an individual expresses one particular point of view vehemently from the beginning, other members of the group will often be reluctant to offer a significant challenge. Much of this will depend on your skill in leading the group and in interpreting the group's responses. This is not the place to go into the details of effective group facilitation (there are plenty of good manuals, usually aimed at trainers, if you're interested). In brief, though, the skilled facilitator should be able to identify possible dissenting views and encourage their expression, even in the face of a dominant personality. In practice, though, you'll often find that the outspoken individual only serves to encourage responses from elsewhere in the group.

Another great advantage is that you can select and structure the groups in a variety of ways. It's often useful simply to select a cross-section of individuals from a range of different sub-groups, so that debate is fired by a range of different perspectives. There are some risks to this, however. If, for instance, you include representatives of varying seniority, you may find that the group is dominated by the more senior staff or that the junior staff are reluctant to express their views. Equally, you may find that, in a group of mixed gender, the men tend to dominate the debate (though I've certainly also known the opposite to be true). Again, this will to some extent reflect the skill of the group leader.

Conversely, it's also sometimes useful for all the members of a particular workshop to come from the same sub-group – from the same department, job-type or grade, for example. This may be particularly helpful where, for instance, you wish to investigate an unexpected response from that group; members can share their different responses to similar experiences. They can debate meaningfully from a shared base of knowledge. And, if you're lucky (or, probably more accurately, if you handle the group sufficiently skilfully), you may even be able to set up, in microcosm, a similar dynamic to that operating in the sub-group as a whole.

This can often be very revealing. If you're puzzled by an unexpectedly negative response from, say, a particular department, discussion may indicate that the group is dominated by a small number of cynical, rather destructive individuals who influence the opinions of the rest. Or, if the response from the department was disproportionately positive compared with the rest of the organization, the group discussion might indicate that the group is heavily influenced by a particularly positive and charismatic supervisor.

As with one-to-one follow-up interviews, group discussions can often be a helpful mechanism not only for providing additional data about the present but also for identifying practical suggestions for the future. You can usually begin by asking a question such as:

> Look, 72% of respondents are unhappy with the way we calculate the current bonus payments. Do you have any thoughts as to how we might improve it?

Once one person comes up with a (perhaps half-hearted) suggestion, someone else will often take it up 'I've often thought we should do it that way. And on top of that we could also . . . ' Before you know it you've got several good suggestions. Or, at the very least, the initial half-hearted suggestion has been refined and developed into a workable idea.

Summary

- Produce a short accessible summary of your findings
- Use interviews and group workshops for follow-up research
- Refine your conclusions in the light of new evidence
- Listen to the extreme and unusual views
- Explore all the grey areas and new hypotheses
- Encourage specific positive suggestions
- Identify the steps which need to be taken.

Chapter Ten

Time for Action

'Great actions speak great minds, and such should govern'

Beaumont and Fletcher, The Prophetess

Some time ago, a colleague and I visited a potential client who was interested in commissioning an employee survey. We had discussed the subject at length and formulated in detail the objectives of the survey. We had also discussed the issue of commitment. The man we were talking to was the Personnel Director of the organization, and he assured us that the proposed survey had the full support of the Chief Executive and the Board. Mindful of the issues we've discussed in this book, we asked, 'They may well be committed to the idea of the survey. But are they really committed to taking the kinds of actions that might be necessary?' 'Oh, I think so,' said the Personnel Director. 'I've considered the issues as realistically as I can. I've spelt out to them what I think we'll probably need to do as a result of the survey. And,' he added, pre-empting our next question, 'I've also spelt out to them the most extreme action that we might have to take if the survey results are worse than we expect. They've assured me that they'll give whatever support is needed to take whatever action we need to take. And I think we can rely on that.'

So that was all right then. We finished our discussion, and just as we were getting up to leave, my colleague suddenly asked, 'Incidentally, is this the first time your organization has conducted an employee survey?'

'The first time? Well, no, actually,' said the Personnel Director. 'We conducted one on roughly the same issues a few years ago.

We used Consult, Invoice and Run, your competitors. They did a very good job, if you don't mind me saying so.'

We stopped at the door. 'What happened as a result of the survey? What were the outcomes?'

'Oh well, we did this,' he said, reaching into his desk drawer and producing a glossy summary report on the survey findings. 'Issued it to all staff. It went down very well.'

'Did it?' we said, walking back into the room. 'And then what happened?'

The Personnel Director blushed slightly. 'Well, we conducted some further research. To see what people thought of the survey and the report.'

'Interesting,' we said. 'And what did they think?'

The Personnel Director looked slightly more relaxed. 'They were very pleased actually. They liked the report. Thought it was clear, easy to read. And they thought that the survey had more or less got things spot on.' He paused. 'Mind you, quite a lot of them expressed some cynicism about whether anything would actually happen as a result of the report . . . '

'And did it?' we asked, simultaneously.

'Well, I suppose it depends what you mean by "happen", really . . . ' He paused again, blushing once more. 'Well, no, actually. Not much. I mean, we meant to, but then things got in the way. We got a new MD, and the new man had other priorities, I suppose. And there were various plans of action, but unfortunately they all kind of petered out. I suppose we were all just too busy . . . '

This experience is far from unusual. Organizations spend considerable (sometimes awe-inspiring) sums of money commissioning complex employee surveys. They prepare very carefully for the exercise. They follow (more or less) all the advice in this book. They bring in the consultants, who spend weeks in the organization, conducting exploratory interviews, designing the questionnaire, carrying out the survey, holding follow-up interviews, producing detailed reports of all the findings.

And then nothing happens.

Of course, it's not always noticeable that nothing's happening. And sometimes it takes months, years even, for nothing to get around to happening. During this period, things *appear* to be going on. There are developments. Meetings are held. Discussion groups are organized. The organization sets up working parties . . .

But still, when you look closely, what's happening is – nothing.

And then, over time, other concerns begin to take precedence. Perhaps the organization's profits are down that year, so there's a sudden panic about cost-efficiency. The senior management get embroiled in restructuring, staff cuts, reinvestment. The Chief Executive leaves and is replaced. There are some changes on the Board. The manager who was championing the exercise is rewarded for his apparent efforts and takes over General Manager for Scotland . . .

And, in the end, nothing has happened. The report – not to mention the glossy summaries and the follow-up reports – languishes untouched on managers' top shelves. Until, perhaps four or five years later, as in the organization cited above, a new set of managers decide that they've identified a further set of issues and decide to hold another employee survey . . .

Jumping the hurdles

This may sound like an exaggeration, but it's quite typical of many cases. Indeed, it's almost over-optimistic. Many employee surveys founder at much earlier stages.

Yet even if you manage to avoid all the major hurdles (and the advice in this book should assist you in doing just that), it's still difficult to ensure that the survey leads to appropriate decisions and actions. After all, even if you've got nominal commitment to taking whatever action is needed, an employee survey will often produce uncomfortable results. It might indicate that you need to scrap or thoroughly redesign the expensive bonus scheme you've only just finished installing. It might indicate that you need to completely overhaul your approach to communications. It might demonstrate that your Chief Executive's much-desired proposal to relocate (coincidentally to a site rather nearer his country home) is a non-starter as far as the employees are concerned.

It's worth remembering that, whatever managers may *say* in opposition to such uncomfortable findings, their real objections will often not be financial at all. In any case, if you've done your preparation properly, they should already have committed themselves to the potential prospect of spending the money needed – although, of course, there's many a slip between a commitment in principle and an action in practice. Yet their real objections will not be financial but political or even emotional. The Personnel Director doesn't object to the scrapping of the bonus scheme because of the cost involved, considerable as it may be. He objects because he's invested an enormous amount of his time, energy and emotional commitment to the scheme, and he's therefore reluctant to let it go, particularly as he also views the survey findings as an implicit criticism of his abilities. And, as you might have guessed, the Chief Executive won't take any notice of the findings on relocation, not because of the cost implications, but because he's really got his heart set on a much shorter journey every morning.

Even if the survey findings aren't particularly uncomfortable, you may still encounter reluctance to take action. Change is always traumatic, and organizations are notoriously resistant to it. And, on occasions, organizations – and the managers who run them – will go to extraordinary lengths to *suggest* activity while not actually doing anything; hence the plethora of further reports, papers, working parties, meetings, etc. that will almost invariably follow any demand for major change, including the findings of an employee survey.

So how do you overcome this inertia? We've said all along that the primary aim of an employee survey should be to improve the quality of management decision-making – but when you've got the data you need, how do you ensure that the decisions actually get taken? If you've followed all the advice in the preceding chapters and you've obtained some useful and revealing findings, how do you ensure that they're acted upon?

As always, there's no simple answer to this question. If you've got the key to guaranteeing organizational change, then throw aside this book instantly and write one of your own – you'll make a fortune. Nevertheless, there *are* some practical steps you can take, both while you're conducting your employee survey and once you've obtained the results, to increase the possibility that action will follow.

Making things happen

The first step is to ensure, from the earliest possible moment, that everyone involved *really* understands the probable and the possible implications of the survey. We've made this point throughout the previous chapters, but it does bear considering in slightly more detail. Firstly, you should ensure that anyone who's likely to be affected is not only aware of the possible implications of the survey, but is aware *in detail* of the potential impact that the findings might have on him or her personally.

In other words, if there's a possibility that the survey might lead to, say, the scrapping of the organization's new bonus scheme, then go along to the Personnel Director (or whoever's appropriate) *as soon* as you're aware that this might happen. Explain the possible implications of the survey as clearly (and as tactfully) as you're able. 'Look,' you say, 'obviously we don't yet know what the results of the survey are likely to be. But I have picked up one or two murmurings of discontent about the bonus scheme. It's occurred to me that one result – admittedly the most extreme we're likely to encounter – would be unanimous opposition to the new scheme. If that happened, it's possible that the Board might decide that it wasn't advisable to continue it. Of course, it'll almost certainly not happen, but if it did, how would you react?'

Once you've got over the cries of 'Over my dead body!' and 'What a ridiculous suggestion!', you'll probably find that the Personnel Director is willing to talk seriously about the possibility. After all, if the worst should come to the worst, it'll be wise to make sure that his or her back's covered. He or she will want to have an appropriate response ready – 'Well, yes, we'd more or less come to the conclusion that our experiment wasn't working, so we've come up with some proposals to change it . . . ' – or at least to start preparing the excuses. Though they almost certainly won't admit it, they'll probably be grateful to you for alerting them to the possibility that such changes may be on the cards.

This kind of discussion has two benefits. First, as we've said, it ensures that those involved are really aware of the potential implications of the survey. And, if you're in any doubt about this, do spell it out. It's astonishing how far people can continue to delude themselves that, despite all warnings, unpleasant consequences won't ensue.

The second benefit is that, by preparing managers for the worst outcome, you're probably making them more receptive to less extreme changes. If you've managed to convince them to devote some thought to the possibility of scrapping the entire bonus scheme, they'll be highly relieved when they only have to amend it slightly. On the other hand, if they'd managed to convince themselves that there would be no change at all, then they'd probably resist vehemently even the most minor adjustments.

This might smack (or reek) of manipulation; I prefer to think of it as good, sound organizational psychology. It's what's sometimes referred to, in the context of negotiation, as 'expectation structuring'. In other words, you're defining the framework within which future discussions will take place. It's the same process you go through when you're selling a second-hand car. In the context of the employee survey, you're signalling to those involved, 'Look, this is a serious matter. It may carry very major implications. You need to think how you're going to respond to those.' And if the consequences turn out to be less extreme than you've suggested, well and good.

Keep people informed

Once you've spoken to all those involved (or potentially involved) about the possible implications of the survey, the next step is to ensure that they *stay* informed. It's surprising how often this doesn't happen. The manager running the survey gets bogged down in the detail and forgets to let his colleagues know what's happening. Of course, there's a management team meeting every month at which the matter's discussed. But, just as a week is a long time in politics, so a month can be an awfully long time in an employee survey.

One of the earliest lessons you learn in consultancy is: never let your conclusions surprise the client. If you do, and if the conclusions are unpleasant ones, there's a very good chance that the client will reject your findings. An effective consultant will endeavour to keep the client aware of progress, informally highlighting any unexpected or unpleasant developments. By the time the consultant comes formally to present the findings, the clients will have a pretty good idea of what to expect and should have reconciled themselves to any unpleasant consequences.

This lesson also holds good for employee surveys. If you end up surprising your colleagues with any unpleasant findings, however minor, you can bet you'll encounter resistance if you propose to take any consequent action. And, quite frankly, you'll deserve resistance. Your colleagues won't have had any opportunity to think through the consequences of your findings, they won't have had any time to prepare their responses (not to mention their excuses), they won't have had any chance to consider alternative options. In this context, you can hardly be surprised if their immediate reaction is to deny the validity of your findings, to challenge the reliability of the survey, or simply to ignore it entirely.

As soon as you spot any factors in the survey which are likely to have wider implications, go *immediately* and discuss them with the relevant people. Don't be nervous about raising the most extreme implications – you'll do nobody any favours by pretending that things are simpler than they are. If, while you're conducting your exploratory interviews, it gradually becomes evident that there is severe dissatisfaction with particular aspects of office accommodation, then go straightaway and talk to all those who would need to be involved in any changes, from the Chief Executive downwards. And, if your preliminary findings seem to justify it, then ask the question, 'What happens if the worst comes to the worst? What happens if we find such severe dissatisfaction with our accommodation that we have to consider fundamental changes – either relocation or complete renovation of our current premises . . . ?'

The initial reaction, as always, will probably be, 'Oh, it'll never come to that, surely . . . ?' And probably it won't, but be persistent anyway: 'Maybe not, but what if it does?'

It almost doesn't matter what the answer to this question is, so long as you persuade your colleagues to think about it. At least they'll have to consider all the possible implications – the costs, the practical problems, the human-resource issues – before they face the final survey findings. If they decide that fundamental change is out of the question, so be it. At least they should be able to argue their case coherently in the face of employee dissatisfaction. If it doesn't come to that, as it very probably won't, they'll be in a much better position to face whatever needs and action-points *do* emerge from the survey.

Ensuring commitment

The third stage, assuming that you've kept all the relevant parties fully informed of the survey's progress, is to ensure continuing commitment to the final survey findings – and, more importantly, to the practical implications of these findings. There's room for at least one more workshop, this time with your senior colleagues.

The precise structure of this workshop will depend on the nature of the survey and your organization. In general, though, this first *implementation workshop* should involve all those senior managers whose commitment is needed actually *to get things done*. In other words, the participants need to be sufficiently senior to drive through the actions to be taken in response to the survey findings.

Quite often, this will be the Board. In other cases, depending on the size of the organization, it may be more junior functional managers. For example, if the survey's findings only really have local implications, it may be more useful to involve, say, the Site Personnel Manager, the local Chief Accountant and so on. But don't make the mistake of pitching the meeting at too junior a level. It's easy to do this, particularly if more senior managers express reluctance to bother themselves with the exercise. But the consequence is that the more junior managers use their bosses as excuses to avoid action.

On the other hand, be careful also not to exclude more junior managers who might have a crucial effect – positive or negative, but especially the latter – on the whole exercise. It's not unusual in many organizations for comparatively junior managers to wield considerable power – particularly the power of veto. I've known large organizations which in practice are run, almost single-handedly, by, say, the Administration Manager. It's not always entirely clear how these individuals have managed to achieve this position of power – though bloody-mindedness and a Services background often seem to help – but there's no doubt of their influence. The Chief Executive will say, 'Well, yes, it's a good idea and I'm all in favour. Mind you, I don't know if old Albert would wear it.

And, after all, he's the one who's got to implement it . . . ' If old Albert won't wear it, then it doesn't happen.

Although you may despise yourself for doing so, if there is a character like this in the organization, then for goodness sake involve him (it's almost always a him) in the implementation workshop. If you don't, you can be sure he'll hinder your progress at every stage. On the other hand, if you've got his support, there'll be very little that you can't achieve!

Preparing for the workshop

The aim of the implementation workshop is to obtain full commitment to the findings of the survey – and, more importantly, to the actions that are needed in response. Once you've prepared your draft findings, circulate these to all the members of the implementation workshop. Highlight those aspects which carry implications for each member. And spell out, as clearly as you can, the actions that you think should follow in each case. But try not to be too dogmatic. It's usually best to employ phraseology such as 'This would seem to suggest that we should, as a matter of some urgency . . . ', rather than 'We therefore must immediately . . . ' Few people like being told what to do – particularly if what they're being told to do is unpleasant. On the other hand, most of us are willing to receive advice, provided we feel free to accept it or reject it as we see fit. Your aim at this stage is simply to ensure that everyone understands the implications; at the workshop, you'll be trying to obtain their commitment.

It's a good idea to go and talk to each of the recipients personally, prior to the workshop. In this way, you can gauge their reactions to the document. You can find out which elements they seem to be happy with and which they're likely to resist. If there are any questions of interpretation, you can resolve these – it's much better to resolve all factual questions at this stage than to get sidetracked at the workshop. If they wish to challenge or question any aspect of the findings, then you can be aware of this. With a bit of luck, you might even be able to answer such challenges there and then. If you can't, at least you can plan your strategy at the workshop accordingly.

In short, you should try to assess individual reaction and resolve individual problems *before* the workshop. The last thing you want is for someone to raise some unexpected objection or query during the meeting itself. At best, this will distract the meeting from achieving its practical objectives. At worst, it might undermine the overall credibility of the survey findings. There's nothing worse than the moment when one of the participants, eager to avoid taking action, says, 'Quite frankly, before we start, I must say I find it very hard to take seriously any report which claims that there are *three* divisions in the production department, when we all know that there are now *four* . . . '

Running the workshop

Before the workshop starts, make your own list of the action points you want to see come out of it. In practical terms, you'll probably need to restrict these to no more than half a dozen – it's a confident manager who expects any organization to take more than six significant actions at any one time. In the case of a survey on relocation, for example, these might be:-

- relocate south of the Trent
- provide full relocation assistance, including a good disturbance allowance
- provide customized support for those with specific problems (e.g., school-age children, aged relatives, etc.)
- provide visits to the proposed area, time off for house hunting, etc.
- provide assistance to working spouses in finding alternative employment.

If the survey really seems to demand more actions than this, then you'll probably just have to prioritize – and either abandon the other action points or postpone them. If they're important, then by all means keep them up your sleeve. You never know, you might find that the meeting agrees to the others more readily than you expect, in which case you might have a chance of getting support for other actions as well. On the other hand, remember that, even if you do get the support of the meeting, this doesn't mean it'll necessarily be translated into action. If you really want to make sure that things get done, it's usually better to keep the exercise tightly focussed.

Your role in the workshop should be to act as a facilitator. Present the key survey findings clearly and succinctly (don't assume, even if you've talked to all the members individually, that they'll necessarily have read the whole report). Outline the aims of the meeting: to achieve commitment to a series of specific action points, to allocate responsibility for implementing them, and to agree timescales for their completion. Once you've done that, you can get down to discussing the report.

In my experience, if you've done your preparation and home-work properly, and if you structure the meeting carefully, you shouldn't have too much difficulty obtaining commitment to your action points. Most of them should, in any case, be pretty much indisputable on the basis of your survey findings. And if you've discovered, during your individual visits to the workshop members, that there's a high level of opposition to a particular idea, you can always quietly drop or amend it. For example, if you discover that nobody's willing to wear the idea of customized relocation packages for those with special needs, then it might be worthwhile to drop this and try instead for a good overall package.

If you know that one or two of the action points are likely to meet with some resistance, but you don't feel able to omit them, leave them till last. Get the straightforward points settled first, and then move on to the trickier ones. You don't want to get distracted into an inconclusive debate and end up with nothing.

Once you've got commitment to the action points (or as many as you're likely to get), it's time to start pinning people down. It's often helpful to set a fixed period for the meeting before you start – and with very senior managers you'll probably have to, anyway. If the participants know that the meeting is going to last, say, two hours and no more, then they're (slightly) less likely to get involved in some open-ended and pointless discussion. Furthermore, when you're half-an-hour before the end, you have an excuse to start drawing the threads of the meeting together.

Concluding the workshop

The simple message is: don't be fobbed off. You'll find that many of the participants, even if they've nominally committed themselves to the action points, will begin to back off when it comes to committing themselves to *action*: 'Oh, I don't think we need to decide that now, do we? My diary's a bit full over the next couple of months, but I'll come back to you with some dates' or 'Well, I don't think I'd better take that on myself. I'll get Peter to come back to you when he's free.'

We all know the excuses, and we all know how easy it is to fall for them. But don't. Your aim is to come out of this meeting with precise commitments from those involved, with deadlines attached. Of course, the allocation of the action points will depend on the nature of the survey and the composition of the meeting. But your aim is not necessarily to get the great and the good to do the work themselves. It's simply to get them to take responsibility for ensuring that it's done.

For example, suppose that the action points are to do with office accommodation. They might be as follows:

- to accept the need for a thorough overhaul of office accommodation
- to prepare detailed comparative estimates of the costs of i) renovating the current accommodation; ii) relocating to leasehold property in the area; or iii) relocating to freehold property in the area
- to prepare a detailed report on the practical implications of the three options
- to prepare a preliminary report on the human-resource implications of relocation.

The first of these is straightforward enough – it can be simply agreed by the meeting. But make sure that there's a formal record of it in the minutes – that might be useful ammunition later. The remaining points can then be allocated as appropriate. For instance, the second and third points might be allocated to the Director of Administration and the fourth to the Director of Personnel. In each case, make sure that this is formally recorded and, even more important, *set a deadline*.

The only problem then is to maintain the initiative. Make sure that the first workshop ends with an agreed date for a follow-up meeting – don't be fobbed off with 'Oh, we can agree that nearer the time . . . ' – and that further follow-up meetings are arranged from then on until you achieve all your practical objectives.

Make things happen!

All the above action points are to do with preparing reports. But don't allow the process to stop there. While there's clearly a need to gather information and to evaluate options, this can easily become an excuse for further procrastination. The organization ends up producing report after report and still nothing happens. If the first workshop concludes with action points aimed at *gathering information*, the second should end with action points aimed at *making decisions*. And the third should end with action points aimed at *implementing the decisions*.

Of course, this is a council of perfection. In practice, unless you're very lucky, the whole process will prove much more frustrating and long-winded. Yet if you do manage to maintain this kind of focus throughout, you're much more likely to achieve practical results than if you allow yourself to be fobbed off with vague promises and uncertain commitments. In my experience, if the commitments are precise and public, peer-group pressure will usually do the rest.

One final point: beware working parties. In my cynical view, one of the unwritten rules of management is that working parties usually do anything but work. They drink coffee. They discuss the issues. They take hours and provide minutes. But they don't produce results. You need the workshop to provide peer-group pressure, so long as you keep it under control. But if any of the workshop members says, 'You know, I thought that rather than undertaking this action point myself, I'd set up a working party in the department to look into it . . . ', then be firm. You should respond, 'Well, fine, Brian, how you do the work's up to you. *Just so long as you produce the results by 29 October as we agreed.*'

Summary

- Be systematic in presenting your findings to the workshop
- Decide on the precise action points you want to achieve
- Involve all those managers whose commitment is needed to *get things done*
- Don't be fobbed off with vague promises
- Obtain commitment to the achievement of precise objectives by specified timescales
- Put it all in writing so you can hold it against them, if necessary
- Be persistent: make sure you've always agreed a date for the next meeting
- Don't let the process get bogged down in information gathering and report writing; drive the meeting as quickly as is practical towards decision-making and action
- Beware of working parties!

A Few Conclusions

'Securus iudicat orbis terrarum'

St Augustine, Contra Epist. Parmen.

It is now worth reviewing some of the main points made in this book. Before you begin to conduct or commission an employee survey, you need to ask yourself the following questions:

- What decisions do we (or might we) really need to make?
- Do we have sufficiently detailed and reliable information about employee attitudes and opinions to make these decisions?
- If not, what kinds of data do we need?
- And, above all, is it likely that an employee survey will provide this information?

Once you've answered these questions to your satisfaction, you can start thinking in detail about your survey. That's when the work really begins, so let's just recap on the cardinal points you need to remember:

- A survey is *not* an easy option. Don't do it just because it seems like a good idea at the time. If you prepare properly, an employee survey can lead to major improvements in the effectiveness of management action, but it'll also prove costly, time-consuming, frustrating and potentially risky
- Think through *all* the possible implications before you commit yourself. Don't just think about the most likely (or, worse still, the most desired) outcomes. Think about the worst

158

possible outcome – once you've committed yourself to a survey, you'll have to go through with it all the way. You'll be raising expectations; if you fail to respond to these, you end up in a worse position than before

• Make sure that *all those who matter* are fully committed to the survey – and to its possible consequences. These will clearly include some of the senior managers, from the Chief Executive downwards, but also relevant line managers as well as employee representatives such as trade unions

• In most cases, an employee survey is much more than merely a written questionnaire. It is a lengthy process, usually involving three key stages. Remember our 'hourglass' model:

Stage 1 – open, participative exploratory interviews to test initial theories and gain a broad, qualitative understanding of the major issues
Stage 2 – a closed, written questionnaire to obtain precise, quantitative data
Stage 3 – a further series of open, participative interviews or workshops to explore and test the issues arising from the written survey

• Although you can certainly try and conduct an employee survey yourself, it's usually better to involve a third-party consultant at least to carry out the central surveying process; you gain the benefits of the consultant's experience and expertise, and employees feel reassured of the survey's confidentiality. (Furthermore, it helps people like me pay the mortgage . . .)

• Once you've collected your data, you need to give very careful thought to what it really means. Keep an open mind and try to avoid jumping to conclusions. If you're not sure of anything or the findings appear contradictory, try to obtain more information through the follow-up sessions.

• Above all, remember that the survey doesn't end when you've collected the data. The only reason to conduct an employee survey is *make the right things happen*. Once you've decided what actions *should* result from the survey findings, pursue these as energetically and systematically as you can.

And that, more or less, is all you need to know. If you follow these guidelines, I can't guarantee that everything will run perfectly. But you should at least succeed in gaining valuable data, making better decisions and, above all, taking more effective action.

Some Suggestions for Further Reading

Roland and Frances Bee, *Management Information Systems and Statistics* (IPM, 1990)

W.A. Belson, *The Design and Understanding of Survey Questions* (Gower, 1981)

D. Mackenzie Davey, D. Rockingham Gill and P. McDonnell, *Attitude Surveys in Industry* (IPM, 1970)

A.N. Oppenheim, *Questionnaire Design and Attitude Measurement* (Heinemann, 1968)

David Parsons, *Employment and Manpower Surveys: A Practitioner's Guide* (Institute of Manpower Studies, 1984)

S. Payne, *The Art of Asking Questions* (Princeton University Press, 1951)

Tom Kynaston Reeves and Don Harper, *Surveys at Work: A Practitioner's Guide* (McGraw-Hill, 1981)

K.A. Yeomans, *Statistics for the Social Scientist: 2, Applied Statistics* (Penguin, 1968)

Index